SCHOLARSHIP AND FREEDOM

SCHOLARSHIP
and
FREEDOM

GEOFFREY GALT HARPHAM

Harvard University Press

CAMBRIDGE, MASSACHUSETTS
LONDON, ENGLAND
2020

Library of Congress Cataloging-in-Publication Data

Names: Harpham, Geoffrey Galt, 1946– author.
Title: Scholarship and freedom / Geoffrey Galt Harpham.
Description: Cambridge, Massachusetts : Harvard University Press,
    2020. | Includes bibliographical references and index.
Identifiers: LCCN 2020008890 | ISBN 9780674245013 (hardcover)
Subjects: LCSH: Du Bois, W. E. B. (William Edward Burghardt),
    1868–1963. | Lategan, Bernard C. | Nochlin, Linda. | Learning
    and scholarship. | Intellectual freedom.
Classification: LCC AZ101 .H37 2020 | DDC 001.2092 / 2—dc23
LC record available at https://lccn.loc.gov/2020008890

For Joel Conarroe

CONTENTS

SCHOLARSHIP AND FREEDOM

Introduction

A Tropism toward Freedom

FOR OVER TWO HUNDRED YEARS, scholarship, which I will define in very loose terms as *an argument about human activity based on a critical examination of evidence,* has been advanced as the most rigorous and reliable means of determining the truth of the human past and thus the best source of knowledge of the human condition. The integrity of scholarship depends on its independence from power, habit, prejudice, desire, or any force external to scholarship. A free discourse that produces freedom, scholarship is free or it is nothing. The formula sounds easy and benign, and yet, as I will try to show, "scholarship and freedom" is more appropriately considered as a set of problems than a solution.

1

Wherever there have been things to learn there have been learned people, but I will be considering only the modern Western form of scholarship, which emerged from older forms of philology, erudition, exegesis, commentary, and historical narrative in the broad context of the European Enlightenment, a philosophical movement predicated on freedom as the key concept in morals, politics, and aesthetics. Modern scholarship is a historically and culturally specific activity that grows out of and supports concepts of personal and political autonomy, responsibility, and accountability. So while the immediate goal of scholarship is to produce knowledge, the real project concerns human freedom.

While these lofty concepts often seem to be glaring in their absence in many of the institutional situations in which scholars actually find themselves, they form the core of the scholarly enterprise. And so the argument I want to explore in what follows is that scholarship and freedom must be grasped together, with freedom understood as the enabling condition and ultimate goal of scholarship, and scholarship as the most refined and disciplined form of the fundamental freedoms of inquiry and expression. When we see matters in this way, I will argue, we understand each term in a richer and more accurate way.

Scholars enjoy many obvious freedoms. They can choose their field, their general area of specialization within that field, and the projects on which they work. Once embarked on that project, they can establish the parameters, select a methodological approach, choose the theoretical premises, set the tone, pick the examples—

everything. Moreover, the scholar is virtually compelled by the protocols of the practice to create an original argument, advancing conclusions not found elsewhere. All scholarship is in this sense "revisionist." Additionally, the actual conduct of scholarly work requires a certain kind of distance from many of the ordinary circumstances of life. Scholarship requires sustained focus; one cannot do it well or even at all if the world presses too closely in on one. To be a scholar, one must pretend, or learn to behave as if, one has the opportunity, the resources, and the personal security to pursue the truth wherever it may be hiding, and to come to honest conclusions even if they challenge one's own prior understandings or values. A vanishingly small number of people are actually in such a position, so the scholarly persona is chosen and performed for the occasion, not given and natural. As the three discussions that follow seek to demonstrate, the character of the individual scholar can be richly revealed, expressed, and extended through his or her work, but scholarship itself involves an act of self-dissociation in which responsibilities, obligations, entanglements, and difficulties of all kinds are suspended so the work may proceed.

The small liberties just listed represent modest forms of a more impressive set of freedoms that, taken together, constitute an inventory of the central values of modernity. The existence of any scholarly work testifies to the fact that the author enjoys the freedom to determine one's own ends or projects, freedom from a master, freedom to choose one's principles, freedom from want and need, and freedom from the hard necessities of nature. Western society has long regarded these freedoms as primary goods and the proper goals of a just political order.

Scholars are granted their freedoms not because they deserve them but because the society that supports scholarship believes that the work they do serves the ends of that political order. The scholarly contribution to freedom need not and even should not be immediate or direct, but a scholarly practice that makes no contribution at all has no claim on society's resources or respect. The overriding goals of scholarship—the emancipation of the mind from falsehood, confusion, misinformation, groupthink, prejudice, habit, the approximations or illusions of received wisdom—are justified only insofar as they contribute in some way to greater public understanding of our limits and capacities, and thus, perhaps, to greater clarity about our prospects and possibilities.

In short, the sense of unworldliness associated with scholarship is enabled by worldly institutions for the purpose of serving worldly ends. As a worldly concept, freedom is never pure or absolute, never found in a feral state, but is always conditioned, restricted, or resisted. What scholars experience as social or institutional encroachments on their freedoms should be seen in this light, not only as irritants or impurities but also as markers of worldliness.

The list of such markers is admittedly substantial. It begins with the protracted apprenticeship in which one learns the necessity of submission to scholarly protocols and deference to the established authorities, and extends to the inordinate amount of work required just to understand the simplest things about a complicated field, the even more inordinate amount of time and effort required to master those things, the treacherous business of venturing even the tiniest alteration in the imposing and credentialed edifice of received wisdom, the uninspiring task of figuring out which scholars one can challenge with impunity and which are untouchable, the staggering commitment to solitary labor involved in supporting the most modest proposals, and, finally, the sobering prospect of a lifetime of such. Added to all this, there is the scholarly profession, which in its ideal form might seem like a model of meritocratic egalitarianism in which all are equal in service to the truth, but which, in its actually existing forms, often resembles and even exemplifies a hierarchical bureaucracy, with offices, ranks, protocols, and a rich array of penalties and punishments for deviation or even idiosyncrasy. Max Weber's famous 1917 lecture "Science as a Vocation" has the status of a timeless classic because of its detailed, unsparing, and sadly evergreen inventory of such conditions.

Scholars submit to these circumstances not always happily but voluntarily, in exchange for the privilege of submitting to other conditions—the discipline of the work, the interest of the materials, the excitement of discovery, and the sense of temporary liberation from the ordinary troubles of life. At the core of scholarship is an assertion of freedom in conditions of chosen constraint, with the implication that the constraints, because they are chosen, confer weight and authority on the assertion. The scholar who can persuade his readers that he has undergone a process of self-mastery and self-dissociation may also be able to persuade them that the truth is speaking through him.* The rules and conventions of scholarship are intended not to eliminate the agency of the author but to cleanse that agency of any merely personal limitations or prejudices that might corrupt the argument. Nobody can achieve perfect hygiene in this respect, so the success of this effort in any given case is open to question, and is in fact one of the leading sources of academic dispute.

Scholarship requires this kind of authority because it consists not of equations or simple statements of fact but of arguments. Without authority, one argument is as good as another, a premise that is utterly anti-scholarly. The quiet, seemingly docile and harmless practice of scholarship constitutes an exercise of authority with an aspiration to dominance. Not only does every scholarly statement implicitly claim to advance on previous scholarship by supplementing, superseding, or supplanting it; every scholarly statement seeks to impose itself on the reader, to challenge whatever the reader already knows or believes, and to propose itself as an improvement. A scholarly argument does not simply add to the reader's fund of information but seeks to alter the reader's understanding, to invade the reader's mind with a commanding display of evidence backed by

---

* I use the masculine pronoun in much of what follows not to endorse but to underscore and ultimately to discredit the historical presumption that the kinds of freedom I will be speaking of are primarily male prerogatives. I trust that the usage will grate on the reader as it did on me, and ask only that the reader continue on to the end of the book.

the personal conviction of the author and buttressed by the authority of the institution of scholarship. The constant mission of scholarship is to force a change in the way the reader thinks. For this reason, scholarship can be seen as a characteristic expression of societies inclined to domination. It cannot be surprising when advocates of other ways of knowing—intuitive, mystical, religious, indigenous, commonsensical, or culture-specific—mount anticolonial resistance to the prestige accorded to scholarship, as some have to Western science.

And yet, aggressivity notwithstanding, scholarship implicitly addresses the reader in a dialogic spirit as a free person who is in many respects fully equivalent to the author: sufficiently interested to read, sufficiently informed and sophisticated to judge, and sufficiently secure in his general position in the world that he can, without risk to himself, entertain unfamiliar and perhaps even unpalatable thoughts in a spirit of responsive curiosity. The implied reader of scholarship is fair-minded and urbane, a serious person who is yet not so invested in his own convictions or preferences that he cannot consider challenges to them. The implied message of scholarship is that the reader—in all likelihood but not necessarily another scholar—has both the capacity to judge the validity of an argument and the willingness to change his mind if the argument passes the test.

With its pretensions to precision, method, rigor, evidence, rationality, and perpetual advancement, modern scholarship has much in common with empirical, mathematics-based science. Like the scientific community, the community implied by scholarship is gated, and reserved for those with the right training, attitudes, credentials, and interests. Both are virtual communities, which is undoubtedly a good thing, for few people would actually choose to live in a community where all inhabitants are both like-minded and constantly struggling for recognition and primacy. But science and scholarship are not the same. One difference, I would argue, is that the gates to the community of scholarship are opened wider than those that restrict access to the scientific community. The competent consumer of science must have scientific training, but the consumer of scholarship may be a non-scholar, and scholarship offers itself ultimately to the human community as a contribution to human self-understanding.

Scholarship reflects certain premises about freedom that are very far from global norms, but the community implied by scholarship has some features that might be considered desirable by many different cultures. These include a recognition of cultural and individual differences, a respect for factors of context and perspective, an acceptance of the necessity of changing one's mind in the face of evidence, an acknowledgment that the task of understanding requires an ongoing exploratory effort, a commitment to dialogue and persuasion, a tolerance for dissent, and a collective investment in the ongoing pursuit of the truth.

Reflecting, exemplifying, and normalizing these premises is the secret project of scholarship, subtending all its various activities. The subject of this book is scholarship in general, but scholarship, like other practices, is insistently particular, so in what follows I will thread my arguments through accounts of three extraordinary careers: those of W. E. B. Du Bois, Bernard Lategan, and Linda Nochlin. Many aspects of the work of Du Bois are widely known, but here I explore the scholarly persona he adopted, very deliberately and with considerable effort, as a way of deploying scholarship in the service of a political agenda. Bernard Lategan, a South African scholar of Biblical hermeneutics, is not as well known as Du Bois in the Anglo-American academy, but his astonishing career, played out in a highly charged political environment, throws a bright light on the crucial topic of evidence in scholarship. And the art historian Linda Nochlin serves here as an exemplary instance of the capacity of scholarship to create, to bring newness into the world.

Freedom meant different things to these scholars, but one thing it did not mean was an unthinking continuance of the status quo. In its drive to innovate, true scholarship is inevitably and invariably disruptive. While scholarship may seem an elite activity pursued by coddled professors, scholarship itself cannot be relied on to serve the interests of the privileged, or the interests of anything other than itself, and displays a tropism toward openness and destabilization: Du Bois turned the methods he learned at Harvard and Berlin against the ruling order in his profession and in society at large; Lategan, having begun life as a highly privileged member of the ruling class, used scholarship at first to consolidate and then to undermine the claims of that class to rule; and Nochlin deployed scholarly methods to batter down the doors keeping women artists and scholars from access to recognition and standing.

The question that hovers over every page of this book is whether scholarship can be sustained in a world very unlike the one in which it emerged and first flourished. Scholarship may not seem like the most important or admirable thing in the world today; it may not seem to exhibit freedom in the vernacular sense at all. But the premises and assumptions that support scholarship, and which it in turn supports, are, I will argue, fundamental to the freedoms associated with the modern world. The larger question, and not just for scholars, is whether a world in which the role of scholarship is diminished, devalued, or compromised is a world we would choose to live in.

CHAPTER ONE

The Scholar as Problem

LATE SUMMER OF 1896, and you, a Negro of modest means but considerable resourcefulness living in Brown's Court in Philadelphia's Seventh Ward, hear a knock on the door. Opening it a crack, you see a small, light-skinned man with a neatly trimmed mustache sporting a cane, gloves, and hat. You have never seen such a figure. He says he has some questions he'd like to ask. Suspicious, but judging him harmless, and almost amused by his ridiculous appearance, his peculiar accent, his nervously excessive display of self-assurance, and an hauteur rarely seen in Brown's Court, you admit him to your domicile and clear a place for him to sit.

Marking boxes in a notebook, he takes you briskly through a series of questions about the age, health, employment, income level, entertainment habits, voting habits, church attendance, diet, conjugal condition, literacy, and birthplace of you and everyone in your family. In half an hour, he is on his way. That man will visit virtually all of the twenty-five hundred households in the Seventh Ward, and will speak with some five thousand persons. He will become an object of curiosity and gossip, and often of distrust and hostility. One of your neighbors will challenge him at the front door: "Are we animals to be dissected and by an unknown Negro at that?"

Soon enough, the stranger is gone. No loss; he never exactly fit in. His prim sententiousness was irritating, and absurd since he himself was living just a few blocks away. But three years later, you hear that a book apparently written by that very person has appeared. You make your way to the newly opened Free Library of Philadelphia on Chestnut Street to examine a copy. It is not an easy read. A history and description of the Seventh Ward, the book is filled with categories, statistics, charts, and lists. There is a complete map of the ward with each house placed in one of five categories. Your house, near Seventh and Lombard, is colored all black: "Vicious and Criminal Classes." The man seems obsessed with "classes," whatever they are. Further careful study reveals that you and many of your more resourceful friends—some talented people among them!—have been grouped at the bottom, in the "submerged tenth," perhaps among the "loafers" or "rascals," although some, admittedly, might fairly be called "Negro criminals."

While recording your brief responses to his questions, he had been taking in and judging everything about you—

your diet, your spending habits, your occupation, your cakewalk parties. He had discovered your secret society, and condemns it here for its "scheming and dishonest officers," one of whom you are, and for the "temptation" it offered "of tinsel and braggadocio." And what's this? He actually describes you and your family! "Lombard Street. Five in family; wife white; living in one room; hard cases; rum and lies; pretended one child was dead in order to get aid." You and your friends are all treated as evidence of "certain peculiar social problems affecting the Negro people." Really?

You think to yourself: If that unknown Negro ever shows his face in Brown's Court again, he will have himself a *serious* problem.[1]

In fact, that man already knew he had a problem. In the evenings of that year, after completing his survey-work for the day, he had been composing an essay he called "Strivings of the Negro People," which he published under the name W. E. B. Du Bois in the *Atlantic Monthly* in August 1897, just after leaving Philadelphia to take up a position at Atlanta University. This essay, retitled "Of Our Spiritual Strivings," became the lead essay in a book published in 1903 called *The Souls of Black Folk*.[2] It began with what he called "an unasked question. . . . How does it feel to be a problem?" (*Souls*, 363).

The author knew how it felt from personal experience. His problem, he writes, had first materialized in a deeply unpleasant episode that occurred when he was ten years old—just "a little thing, away up in the hills of New

FIGURE 1. W. E. B. Du Bois, 1900, *courtesy of Special Collections and University Archives, W. E. B. Du Bois Library, University of Massachusetts Amherst.*

England," one of a few dozen people of African descent living among the five thousand residents of Great Barrington, Massachusetts—and a white girl rejected his visiting card "peremptorily, with a glance" (*Souls*, 363). This, he says, was the first indication that he was "different from the others" and "shut out from their world by a vast veil" (364).[3] Thus was born a "peculiar sensation" of "double-consciousness" that he had never since shaken, and that he regarded now as a symptom of a far deeper disorder, one shared by all who must struggle to be both Negroes and Americans. "One ever feels," he wrote, referring both to himself and to all Negroes, "his two-ness," with "two souls, two thoughts, two unreconciled strivings, two warring ideals in one dark body" (364–65).

What precisely was the problem? Du Bois's argument was startling in its originality and sophistication. Two generations after the Civil War, he said, it was still all but impossible for a black man to be both a presumptively free and equal American and a presumptively constrained and inferior Negro. All Negroes, he said, found themselves in an invisible "prison-house," condemned to silent and ineffectual hatred of "the pale world about them," compelled to "plod darkly on in resignation, or beat unavailing palms against the stone, or steadily, half hopelessly, watch the streak of blue above" (*Souls*, 364).

In years to come, these phrases would make Du Bois famous, cited endlessly for their radical new way of thinking about race in America, from the perspective of the unwilling inheritor of a national culture in which the practice of chattel slavery had long been embraced by many and tolerated by most citizens, the nation's professed democratic ideals notwithstanding.

But was Du Bois really thinking only about race when he wrote those sentences? Was he even thinking about race at all? Surely everyone regardless of color feels that they have multiple identities or commitments that are sometimes difficult to harmonize. Double consciousness has been described as "the defining condition of modernity itself,"[4] but was that the source of most black people's problems? How many Negroes at the time were vexed by unreconciled strivings? Would that man in Brown's Court have felt his heart swelling with indignation on hearing about the rejection of the visiting card? Would he have regarded a metaphorical prison as the most immediate threat to his well-being? In a recent book, the historian Sean Wilentz asks, "What did the vast majority of American blacks, still living in the rural South in 1903, know of unasked questions, or of existing as a problem, or of any kind of two-ness at all? Identity, for them, as post-Reconstruction white supremacy reached its zenith, was fixed by the all too straightforward realities of Southern racism, violence, and poverty. Their collective identity owed little enough to the white man's world, or to any complicated refraction of it."[5] Wilentz all but says outright that Du Bois is speaking more directly about himself and people like himself—educated, ambitious, culturally sophisticated; members of the "talented tenth," as he put it[6]—than about black people in general.

Du Bois encouraged a reading in which he figures as the subject as well as the author of the essay, writing in the

"Forethought" to *Souls* that "I who speak here am bone of the bone and flesh of the flesh of them that live within the veil" (*Souls*, 360). Like everyone, Du Bois was a member of many groups. If he is, as Wilentz suggests, not speaking directly in this essay about the experience of being black and American, what is he speaking of? Is it possible he is referring to some other kind of problematic identity— perhaps that of his chosen and fiercely embraced vocation—and that the real problem, for him, was how to be both the object and the subject of knowledge? Such a reading would cast Du Bois not just as a representative Negro but also as the anguished voice of scholarship, exemplifying and even performing in extraordinarily vivid ways some aspects of the scholarly profession that are normally seen and experienced in muted and routinized forms.

With such outsized gifts of intellect, imagination, discipline, and tenacity, why did Du Bois want to become a scholar? Not an obvious or easy career path for anyone, scholarship was an elaborately indirect way for a person to rise in the world, requiring long years of education followed by more years of apprentice labor with uncertain prospects of eventual success. The professions in general offered restricted possibilities for any African American, but the profession of scholarship was more restricted than most inasmuch as it was open primarily to white Christian men of a certain class. Moreover, Du Bois knew that while he might be admitted to college and even graduate school, he could never be employed at any institution other than what is now known as a "historically black college or university," and would never be fully accepted into the elite upper tiers of the academy. So what was the appeal?

The root of the answer is revealed in "Of Our Spiritual Strivings": knowledge is power, beginning with the power to determine one's own fate. Still smarting from the visiting card debacle, the young Du Bois determined to "beat my mates at examination time," demonstrating—since grades were given and recorded for all students regardless of race—his superiority in a manner that could not be denied (*Souls,* 364). This kind of power proved addictive. Determined to go to Harvard but finding that he could not be admitted directly, he went in 1885 to Fisk University in Nashville with the financial assistance of a group of area white citizens who recognized his exceptional promise. Three years later he was admitted to Harvard, where he obtained an undergraduate degree. He went on to the graduate school, and, in 1895, received the first PhD Harvard awarded to an African American.

The world owes that girl, and those citizens, an immense debt of gratitude. Her rejection, which struck Du Bois, perhaps correctly, as a racial insult, gave him his life's mission; and their support enabled Du Bois to train for one of the most influential scholarly careers—one of the most impressive careers of any kind—of his long era.

The power associated with knowledge, particularly in its developed form of scholarship, was not merely personal. As Du Bois recognized early on, knowledge could be socially disruptive, even transformative to a society whose views and values were based on ignorance. He determined to escape the prison-house of prejudice not by denying or ignoring his racial identity but by embracing it, concentrating what he called "the Negro problem" in himself and using his own achievements and growing distinction to address it. In that first chapter of *The Souls of Black Folk,* we can actually see the precipitation of an individual from the anonymous and oppressed mass of "the American Negro." The chapter is titled "Of Our Spiritual Strivings," but the first-person plural occasionally and revealingly resolves into a third-person singular. Imagining a new "ideal of liberty" after the failure of Reconstruction, a "bewildered serf" is depicted in the act of realizing the power of "'book-learning'; the curiosity, born of compulsory ignorance, to know and test the power of the cabalistic letters of the white man, the longing to know. . . . In those somber forests of his striving his own soul rose before him, and he saw himself—darkly as through a veil; and yet he saw in himself some faint revelation of his power, of his mission. He began to have a dim feeling that, to attain his place in the world, he must be himself, and not another" (367–68). That bewildered serf was in fact the author, at that moment emerging out of the tragic centuries of African American history in the United States into articulate self-determining maturity. The souls of black folk would finally come to proud countenance in the striving soul of Du Bois himself, and would do so through the emancipatory instrument of scholarship. To become a scholar was to become self-defining, self-governing, self-determining, a man in full. In his autobiographical novel *Darkwater,* Du Bois recalls his state of mind as he launched his academic career: "I was captain of my soul and master of my fate! I *willed* to do! It was done. I *wished!* The wish came true."[7]

Du Bois folded his considerable personal aspirations into the larger project of advancing the cause of social justice for African Americans. He saw education as a general good, enabling educated African Americans to rise to the level of their abilities, their success constituting a powerful argument for equal opportunity for all.[8] But beyond this specific need for Negro education, Du Bois saw a crying need for the scholarship he was determined to provide. The general dissemination of factual knowledge about the history and current condition of black people would support arguments for the removal of what he called "the greatest and most discouraging obstacle in our paths . . . that unreasoning and unreasonable prejudice of this nation, which persists in rating the ignorant and vicious white man above the intelligent and striving Colored man, under any and all circumstances."[9] The free circulation of ideas would always find favor in a dynamic, future-oriented society, while the insistence on accurate knowledge would ground thinking in reality. "My vision was becoming clearer," he writes in a widely cited passage in *The Autobiography of W. E. B. Du Bois,* which he composed near the end of his life: "The Negro problem was in my mind a matter of systematic investigation and intelligent understanding. The world was thinking wrong about race, because it did not know. The ultimate evil was stupidity. The cure for it was knowledge based on scientific investigation" (197).

A noble goal; but as Du Bois knew, and as countless others have attested, in addition to suffering from the Negro problem, he had a problematic character. Aloof, distrustful, defensive, uncomfortably self-conscious, vain, he was far easier to admire than to like. Some sense of his worldly comportment can be gleaned from an anecdote told by the historian John Hope Franklin, who could be considered Du Bois's successor as the preeminent African American scholar of his era, the most distinguished historian of the African American experience. The two met in 1939, when the twenty-four-year-old Franklin—who would, like Du Bois, live well into his tenth decade—spotted Du Bois dining alone in a Raleigh hotel. Franklin introduced himself, giving his full name. Surely, Franklin thought, Du Bois would respond to the fact that the young stranger had been named after one of Du Bois's closest friends, John Hope, the president of Atlanta University, who had worked with Du Bois in the founding of the Niagara Movement and, subsequently, the National Association for the Advancement of Colored People: "He did not even look up. Then I told him that I was a graduate of Fisk University, class of 1935. That, I assumed, would bring him to his feet singing 'Gold and Blue.' Again, he continued to read and eat, without looking up. Finally, as a last resort, I told him that I was a graduate student in history at Harvard. . . . Without looking up from his book or plate, he said, 'How do you do.'"[10] Du Bois was never going to cease being a problem in some contexts, but in becoming a scholar he was trading one kind of problem for another, superior kind. As a scholar, he would not *have* a problem, he would *be* a problem for those responsible for creating his problem. He would acquire credentials and, in time, reputation and influence far greater than anything an African American man, or indeed any person, might reasonably have aspired to in American society of that time. His existence would be a standing rebuke to those who blocked his path to advancement.

Once admitted to Harvard, Du Bois set about becoming not just well educated but one of the best educated and academically trained people in the country. He studied with William James (with whom he paid a visit to Helen Keller), George Santayana, George Lyman Kittridge, and Josiah Royce. By the time he finished his undergraduate degree, he had studied philosophy, economics, history, political economy, political science, chemistry, psychology, mathematics, Latin, Greek, and literature—the field of sociology not yet having been invented—with some of the most eminent scholars in the country. He then obtained support for two years at the University of Berlin, easily the most prestigious research university in the world, where, from 1893 to 1895, he studied directly with some of the great minds of Europe and attended lectures by Max Weber.[11] At Berlin, he acquired, in addition to knowledge in several fields, an understanding of the principles of scholarship, in which that university had a long history of preeminence. He learned the habits of mind, the patterns of responsiveness, the moral character, and the general outlook and demeanor that a scholar had to possess. He learned how to comport himself in the halls of academe.

When Du Bois arrived in Berlin, the profession of scholarship was still dominated by a positivistic notion of science and scientific objectivity, although, as we will see, cracks in the edifice of certainty had begun to appear. From today's perspective, the academic milieu of much of the nineteenth century seems intellectually crude, its faith in objectivity naïve, its confidence in rationality almost irrational. In *That Noble Dream: The "Objectivity Question" and the American Historical Profession,* Peter Novick describes bluntly as "a cult" the dominance over scholarship of a now-discredited concept of fact.[12] But like cults generally, the profession of scholarship could be tremendously compelling to those on the inside, especially to anyone who, like Du Bois, was young, inexperienced, eager, insecure, impressionable, and grateful for having been admitted.

The sense of method Du Bois would have absorbed from his Berlin professors was based, first, on an uncompromising commitment to the labor of research—comprehensive knowledge, accurate observation, responsible analysis, and the faithful representation of empirically observable fact. Methods of investigation were to be clearly articulated, refined, monitored, and conducted by a community of professionals dedicated to this task and heeding no other imperative than the pursuit of truth. A strict scholarly ethic, an "altruism of the intellect," entailed a total commitment to the truth no matter how difficult to obtain or unpleasant to contemplate.[13] The true scholar was committed to a selfless immersion in the necessities of the work and a principled disregard for convenience, efficiency, ultimate meaning or value, implications, or utilities; such a scholar would reject "peremptorily, with a glance" the manifold pleasures of self-confirmation obtainable through a loose reading of the evidence. Scholars were no respecters of persons, and a community of scholars constituted in principle a perfect democracy in which any marker of rank, status, or privilege was held to be irrelevant at best, an impediment or corruption at worst.

Since these principles were hardly to be found in the world at large, the scholar had to be a certain kind of person. One of Du Bois's professors, Wilhelm Dilthey, was a particularly compelling example of the scholarly character. In the words of one of his students, Dilthey had "no thought whatsoever for his own person"; even to those who knew him well, "'Dilthey' was almost synonymous with 'Dilthey's work.'"[14] Within Dilthey's orbit, any kind of methodological individualism or idiosyncrasy was sharply discouraged. The values, beliefs, wishes, habits, or preferences of the scholar, if he had any, had no legitimate role in the investigation or representation of the facts. Since the facts—the material or especially the documentary traces left by the past—could not speak for or explain themselves, the scholar had to be scrupulously neutral in speaking for them, and any conclusions reached by the scholar had to follow from empirical observations.

This insistence on a voluntary neutralization of the self was supported by the lingering influence in what became known as the Historical School of Leopold von Ranke, a professor at Berlin for over half a century beginning in 1825, and justly regarded as the founder of the modern discipline of academic historiography. It was Ranke who established selfless commitment to arduous labor as the indispensable characteristic of the scholar, and painstaking archival research as the fundamental activity of scholarship. "Let no one pity a man who devotes himself to studies apparently so dry, and neglects for them the delights of many a joyous day," he wrote. "It is true that the companions of his solitary hours are but lifeless paper, but they are the remnants of the life of past ages."[15]

Ranke argued, through aphorism and example, that history could aspire to the status of a science if it severely restricted the influence on the work of general ideas or concepts, eliminated all value judgments, and confined itself to the evidence provided by primary documents. In his most famously compressed statement of principle, he declared that the historian must try to tell "wie es eigentlich gewesen," which is commonly if somewhat misleadingly translated into vernacular English as "how it actually was."[16] The key word, of course, is actually, as opposed to probably or possibly. The scholar was the discoverer, not the creator, of the truth. He could not impose a desirable or satisfying explanation on the evidence or draw moral conclusions from the data of history.

These principles were unquestioned at Berlin. As Du Bois wrote in his lecture notes at the time, "My school tries as far as possible to leave the *Sollen* [should be] for a later stage and study the *Geschehen* [what is actual] as other sciences have done."[17]

Du Bois clearly found the concept of an impersonal practice of scholarship—like residency in Germany, where his race was not held against him—liberating. As a scholar on the German model, he could shed his chronic sense of insecurity and expand to his true dimensions. He went all in. The dissertation he was then writing was an extreme example of the commitment to fact, being based on an exhaustive survey of primary documents—royal edicts, parliamentary and colonial proceedings, federal and state acts and statutes, census tabulations, court decisions, naval reports, bills of lading, and newspaper accounts. This project, published in 1896 as *The Suppression of the African Slave-Trade to the United States of America, 1638–1870*,[18] with nearly 150 pages of appendices, was constructed, as Du Bois would say in the preface, on "the general principles laid down in German universities" (3). By the time it appeared in 1896, Du Bois was deeply involved in *The Philadelphia Negro*, a compellingly original example of the new empiricism then transforming the social sciences, and widely considered the first scientific study of urban African Americans.[19] Once relocated to Atlanta University in 1897, he planned a recurring cycle of ten studies in succeeding decades, the Atlanta University Studies, with all ten repeated in each decade—a full century of collective scholarly labor, the goal of which would be to amass such a quantity of fact that the world would be compelled to renounce its errors with respect to Negroes, and to think better.[20]

Du Bois discovered in German principles a way to contribute to the advancement of his race, and, not incidentally, to advance his own career. He could realize his personal ambitions by engaging in a socially accepted and even honored form of self-neutralization in the service of the truth, and, through a psychic maneuver peculiar to scholarship, fulfill himself by merging with his subject. Scholarship actually allowed for this. In the Berlin context, the notion that a scholar would claim that he was bone of the bone and flesh of the flesh of the object of his research was not as peculiar as it may have been in a more strictly scientific context. As one of his most imposing professors at Berlin, Heinrich von Treitschke, said, the scholar "must forget his own I and feel himself a member of the whole."[21]

The theory was that, purged of its merely contingent features, the enlarged and focused scholarly "I" would become purified, refined, supple, resistant to temptations and distractions, and perfectly responsive to the evidence. As the great German philologist Erich Auerbach said near the conclusion to his 1946 masterwork, *Mimesis: The Representation of Reality in Western Literature*, the process of scholarly understanding works on both the material and the mind. Exiled to Istanbul during the war, and removed from the great research libraries of Germany—if not from those of Istanbul, which he chose not to use—Auerbach had adopted a non-methodical method of "letting myself be guided" in the process of composition by a few motifs he had previously worked out, in the faith that his long training as a scholar had so shaped his mental habits that intuition and informed hunches would lead him to the truth. As he put it, "There is always going on within us"—especially us scholars—"a process of formulation and interpretation whose subject matter is our own self."[22]

Having submitted to this chastening process of depersonalization, the scholar was a superior person; or rather, the scholar was a person who had managed to incubate within himself a second and superior form of personhood that responded only to the imperatives of scholarship and ignored the organic, psychological, and social forces that drove the ordinary person. Open to the past and steeled against the present, the self-mastering scholar was impervious to praise and blame alike. He was not buffeted about by the winds of opinion, not constrained by social limitations, not a mere passive relay for the replication of the prevailing ideology, not addicted to routine, not obsessed by fixed ideas or determined preferences. The scholar was free. All this had an obvious appeal for Du Bois. The American Negro might be limited in various humiliating ways, but a Negro who had trained to become a scholar had achieved a form of emancipation that could not be challenged or revoked.

This account of the ethos at Berlin may make it sound like a kind of monastery, where monks or nuns lived within the strict dictates of a depersonalizing Rule. The analogy is not altogether misplaced. Ranke's discourse has more than a trace of saintly asceticism. The discipline of the scholar as the Historical School conceived it resembled in important ways that of the saintly person, who abandoned the life of society and denied the demands of the body, departing from "the world" in order to construct a life of perfect obedience and freedom, a life lived not for its own sake but for the sake of God. In the nineteenth century and even beyond, many universities described themselves in para-religious terms as a space apart from the world, a unique way of life devoted to the higher cause of learning. Wilhelm von Humboldt, the founder of the University of

Berlin, wrote that in the research university, "the teacher is not there for the students' sake; rather, they are all there for scholarship and knowledge's sake."[23]

The monastic analogy is also illuminating in another respect. The foundational text for Christian asceticism is "If you would be perfect, go, sell what you possess and give to the poor, and you will have treasure in heaven; and come, follow me" (Matt. 19:21).[24] In the religious context, the exhilarating prospect of "treasure in heaven" fortifies the ascetic for the struggle by promising an extraordinary reward that will be granted later and elsewhere. But as Peter Brown has shown, the ascetic heroes of Late Antiquity actually acquired power of a quite literal kind in the here and now, deciding disputes, canceling debts, and generally exerting social force.[25] Similarly, the scholarly ascetic did not have to die in order to enjoy the fruits of his labors. For the giants of the Historical School, the "later stage" Du Bois mentions, when Geschehen yields at last to Sollen and the righteous scholar is free to instruct the world, arrived well before the scholar met his maker. Several of Du Bois's professors had political careers in addition to their academic careers, and others fully expected that their work would influence the administration of the state.[26]

It has become conventional to associate scholarship with an emasculated indifference to the world, as though George Eliot's Rev. Mr. Casaubon were a pure realization of the scholarly ethos. This convention is richly evoked in a book about the popular representation of scholars and scholarship by A. D. Nuttall with the disturbing title *Dead from the Waist Down*, which begins with the comment that, in popular culture, "we have come to expect that the intellectual of the group will be shorter, thinner, and weaker than the others and have less immediate pull for the opposite sex."[27] But this was certainly not how Du Bois saw himself—he spent much of his life making up for that rejected visiting card—and it was definitely not the ethos at Berlin during his time there.

To be a professor at the University of Berlin was to be a man of significance who had every reason to expect that his opinions would be taken very seriously. Nor were these opinions ventured with any perceptible reluctance. On one occasion, Du Bois was sitting in the classroom when von Treitschke—described by Du Bois as a "fire-eating pan-German," "the German Machiavelli . . . the very embodiment of united monarchical, armed Germany," and by David Levering Lewis as "a volcanic bigot of encyclopedic learning"—suddenly opened fire on one of nation's highest officials, calling him a "verrückte Dummkopf" (mad idiot).[28] Max Weber, who was notable even in the German context for his devotion to learning, was perfectly capable of unleashing diatribes, as when he denounced "the masterless slavery in which capitalism enmeshes the worker or the debtor."[29] Another of Du Bois's professors, Gustav von Schmoller, struck Du Bois as a man of radical prejudices against, for example, "morally reprehensible forms of trade" who felt perfectly within his rights to lecture the government on its "moral duty to alleviate undue hardships."[30] All the Berlin faculty seemed to despise something, whether practices, policies, or persons dead or alive. Schmoller's hated Berlin rival Adolf Wagner held Adam

Smith (pronounced, with a sneer, "Adahm Smiss") in perfect, public, and often-reiterated contempt.[31] Taken together, Du Bois's professors at Berlin constitute a veritable gallery of *odium scholasticum,* "scholastic hatred."[32] And yet, none of these sharply etched, venomous, and opinionated individuals questioned the premise that scholarship was a disinterested search for truth.

The rigors of scholarship were also rewarded by another kind of treasure that Du Bois would have coveted. In order to make any sense of the vast unsorted data of the historical record, a scholar required general or theoretical ideas. His stern emphasis on documented particulars notwithstanding, Ranke himself warned against an excessive attention to archival detail that might cause the scholar to lose sight of "the subject as a whole."[33] In the practice of scholarship, general concepts, while dangerous, were regarded as necessary and even, if confirmable, as crowning achievements. After vast toil, the diligent scholar might be able to discern, at the end of the rainbow, the patterns or regularities invisible to the casual observer that gave form and coherence to an entire complex field. The ability to identify and articulate these general concepts—Émile Durkheim's distinction between "sacred" and "profane" was a prominent and controversial example—was the basis for the scholar's authority, and the special glory of Berlin. From its founding, the University of Berlin had been home to great theorizers, especially on the subjects of language, race, and nation.

Nearly ninety years after the founding of the university, these were still considered urgent topics. But by the fin de siècle, when Du Bois was in residency, German romantic notions about race and nation had matured into a rancid and, as history would soon enough demonstrate, sinister decadence. Du Bois was directly exposed to the senescent forms of once-inspiring ideas.[34] He was seated before von Treitschke when the great man suddenly interrupted his lecture on America to declare, "Die Mulattin sind niedrig! Sie fuhlen sich niedrig" (Mulattoes are inferior! They feel themselves inferior) (*Autobiography*, 104). Dazzled by von Treitschke's erudition and fervor, Du Bois managed to avoid taking this tirade personally. Race and nation were already his subjects, and he was deeply interested in the ways in which these were engaged in a non-American context. "Yet von Treitschke was not a narrow man," Du Bois wrote at the time, in terms he might have applied to himself. "His outlook is that of the born aristocrat who has something of the Carlyle contempt of leveling democracy" (*Autobiography*, 104).

For all their aspirations to the dispassionate gathering and recording of fact, then, the distinguished scholars at Berlin did not consider themselves mere drones whose personal views, dispositions, or interests could only be an impediment to their work. They saw themselves in quite different terms, as people whose exceptional learning and discipline qualified them to pronounce on moral and political issues. To the scholar of the human world, ideas, ideologies, and values were themselves historical facts, and the scholar who wished to understand them could not deny their influence over his own thinking. It was, in fact, the scholar's rich inner life that gave him access to the inner life of the past, the inner coherence of a work, the inner form of events.

These, at least, were the terms and the arguments being worked out at Berlin by Dilthey during Du Bois's time there. Dilthey was developing, in sprawling but fragmentary and provisional form, a theory of the human sciences, or Geisteswissenschaften, that built on but also brought into question the fetishization of facts associated with Ranke. In Dilthey's work we can see scholarship, which studied the human world, detaching itself, with great reluctance, from natural science and beginning to establish its own identity. Much of the theoretical work of this disambiguation followed from a single crucial distinction. While events in the natural world, according to Dilthey, could be adequately explained, events in the human world required a different approach that was best described as *verstehen,* generally translated as understanding. The truth of human events could not be expressed in numbers, symbols, or formulae. The past could not be studied as if it were a freestanding object or as the consequence of a simple chain of cause and effect, but had to be apprehended through an act of sympathetic inner apprehension, a re-experiencing by the scholar of the original historical experience.

Dilthey professed great disdain for romantic caprice and subjectivity in interpretation, but he also occasionally confessed to an intuition that never troubled Ranke, that life was unfathomable, dark, and uncanny. Against these forces, the scholar of the human sciences—corruptible, se-ducible, and sensitive to subterranean turbulence as he may be, considered as an individual—counterposed the rules of exegesis. If the scholar followed the proper methods, he might be able to produce what Dilthey in-sisted on describing as a *"scientific* knowledge" of human beings and their works that possessed general or objective validity.[35] Dilthey's work consisted largely of attempts to chart the progress since antiquity toward a codification of those rules of understanding, and to advance the project by providing greater clarity than his predecessors.

Du Bois undoubtedly found Dilthey's seminar inspiring on many levels. Having already committed himself to the premise that accurate knowledge could serve as an anti-dote to racism and a weapon against injustice, Du Bois would have been fortified by Dilthey's confidence about the prospects of an objectively valid science of human events. Du Bois might also have found himself nodding vigorously in agreement with the proposition that the goal of historical knowledge was an inner understanding: as bone of the bone and flesh of the flesh of his subject, he had privileged access to the historical experience and even to the soul of black folk. Du Bois might also have been excited by what others often found confusing, frustrating, or even counterproductive, Dilthey's insistence that understanding could become scientific through the development of an "art of interpretation," a creative construction by the scholar based on a "congenial empathy with the inner soul of other peoples and ages" that Dilthey could only attribute to "personal skill and virtuosity" ("Rise of Hermeneutics,"

233, 240). Bursting with ambition and talent, and driven by the need to prove himself, Du Bois must have felt within himself the volcanic rumblings of just such virtuosity, and the assurance that the exercise of his personal gifts would not compromise the validity of his research must have been deeply welcome.

Du Bois might also have found his own tendencies confirmed by Dilthey's acknowledgment that narrative was the vehicle for conveying an understanding of historical events.[36] According to Lionel Gossman, the status of narrative as the vehicle for understanding the truth of the past became precarious when, in the late seventeenth century, a distinction was drawn between history and fiction.[37] Once drawn, this distinction seemed to rule out the possibility that a truly scientific discourse of history could take the literary form of narrative. The strongest effect was felt in fields such as sociology that aspired to the status of a science. At the beginning of the twentieth century, the polymath Lester Frank Ward spoke for many when he characterized the newly constituted discipline of sociology as "a field of phenomena produced by true natural forces and conforming to uniform laws" as invariant as the laws of gravitation, chemical affinity, or organic growth.[38] For Ward and many like him, narrative was simply too subjective and imprecise a mode to register or represent the "phenomena" sociology sought to analyze.

Recognizing the dominance of science, Ranke and his successors thought that strict adherence to the rules could neutralize the danger represented by subjectivity to the point where a discipline that represented its findings in

narrative form could still qualify as a science. This concession gave Du Bois an opening and a license. He had a story
to tell, and narrative gave him many ways to shape his arguments. The narrator could select and arrange the elements, describe them in a way that gave them coherence,
create causal linkages, clarify lines of force, relegate the irrelevant to the side-spaces, and generally bring things
into their proper relation. Above all, the narrator was an
omnipresent judge and evaluator whose opinions took
forms ranging from deceptively neutral characterization
and description to overt sermonizing, even to the point of
hand-delivering the moral of the story. Du Bois exercised
the narrator's right to judge with an undisguised zeal. He
was particularly drawn to narratives with well-defined
characters, a coherent plot, and a clear point of view—
narratives informed by what Gossman describes as the
"liberal assumption" that "men make their own destinies,
[and] ultimately that history is the story of liberty."[39]

Especially given the preliminary character of Dilthey's
reflections,[40] it is tempting to regard the scholars of the Historical School as primitive figures, immense forms
striding the earth who, in their heroic innocence, regarded
scholarship not as a limited practice of research and inquiry
but as the highest form of cognition itself—at once scientific and intuitive, empirical and imaginative, disinterested
and engaged, value-neutral and morally committed. Their
sense of self-importance may seem to us absurd, and their
theoretical debates niggling, abstract, unresolved, and finally trivial. It is easy to persuade ourselves that we have
progressed well beyond these engorged and disorderly fig-

ures and have achieved a drier, more reliable, reasonable, and modern form of scholarship. But it would be more accurate to regard them as caricatures, unembarrassed examples of a more general conception of scholarship that has outlasted the debates swirling around Berlin at the turn of the century and that continues to the present day.

In this less theoretical and more durable conception—the durability deriving in part from a certain irresolution in the theory—scholarship is a practice that aspires to discover and represent the truth of the past in a manner distinct both from empirical science and from fiction, opinion, or dogma. This practice requires learning and industry, a keen sense of fact, and an uncompromising commitment to discovering and representing the facts in good faith. In addition to this, however, the scholar is also charged with another responsibility, of giving a sense of the meaning, value, essence, significance, proper context, or true form of the facts. To get at this something more, virtues other than erudition and indefatigability are required.

To apprehend the truth of things, the scholar must somehow think his way back into the scene of history to probe the causes, motivations, or intentions behind the events he is studying. An ability to suspend, however provisionally or imperfectly, one's own identity in order to see the world from the perspective of historical actors is a key component of the scholarly character. But since the real determinants of action necessarily lie beyond the mental horizon of the historical actors themselves, the scholar must also adopt a perspective beyond the events described, a perspective not available to any of the participants. This requires not just self-nullifying empathy but also a virtuosic capacity for imaginative speculation. Inference is not observation, a narrative must be constructed out of diverse materials, and judgment is involved at every point in the construction of an argument.

Once the right to judge has been earned, it must be exercised. There is no point in possessing the freedom to judge if that freedom is not put to work in the service of truth, and the indifference to self-ends and the legitimate demands of the world that had isolated and sustained the scholar through long years of toil could only be justified by the scholar's publication of his conclusions. If the minister was, in the honest judgment of the scholar, a *verrückte Dummkopf*, the scholar was compelled by a professional ethic to say as much. *The Philadelphia Negro* contains many empirically true statements about life in the Seventh Ward and the history behind it, but it would, Du Bois appears to believe, be a less truthful book if it merely listed statistics without speaking directly about the rascals, loafers, and criminals he met there, and their wasteful, licentious, and self-destructive ways. The force of truth would also be blunted if the reader was not challenged with difficult questions such as "How long can a city teach its black children that the road to success is to have a white face . . . and escape the inevitable penalty?"[41] In Du Bois's view, which was, on the evidence, not inconsistent with the practice in Berlin, assiduous research precedes, supports, and, most important, *demands* this enhanced and rhetorical form of truth-telling. The truth may be more enhanced and more rhetorical in Du Bois than in most other scholars, but the difference is one of degree not kind.

The scholar's humility before the future is, then, matched and countered by a necessary pride, even arrogance. Because the truth of the past requires his mediation in order to be known at all, and because the world only knows what the scholar tells it, even the most modest scholar is potentially a figure of considerable power. In the seventeenth century, A. D. Nuttall notes, "scholarship was seen as magical," and therefore deeply threatening to a community organized around religious faith (*Dead from the Waist Down,* ix). In the nineteenth century, the learned philologist—whose uncanny researches extended back into the mists of time, all the way back to the point where the original thought-forms of humanity might be glimpsed—was a figure of immense charisma. As Edward Said says with a guarded admiration, "There is an unmistakable aura of power about the philologist."[42] The scholar stands on, or even bestrides, the margin dividing Geschehen from Sollen, and the extent and nature of his ambiguous authority cannot be attributed solely to his command of facts.

The bipolar discipline of scholarship—documentable facts plus something more that gives those facts meaning—enjoins a corresponding bipolarity in the scholar. On this point, the example of Du Bois is most instructive. If the learned bigots, aristocrats, and moralizers of the Historical School seem feral caricatures of modern scholarship, Du

Bois was a caricature of that caricature. An exceptionally committed researcher who believed in the possibility of objective truth, a literary artist and a thundering moralist, Du Bois produced work marked by what Appiah calls "whiplashing shifts of register" from statistics to poetic evocations, from lists to narrative scenes of operatic intensity, from charts to jeremiads (*Lines of Descent*, 80). Indeed, one of Du Bois's friends remarked on the strange character of a man who could be so exacting in his scholarship and yet have a mind cast in such "a weird and fantastic mold."[43] *The Suppression of the African Slave-Trade* is a work of assiduous research marbled throughout with judgments, the book ending not with the suppression of the slave trade but with "The Lesson for Americans," a final section that delivers the goods for those who might have failed to grasp the message. So, too, with *The Philadelphia Negro*, a "great, schizoid monograph," as David Levering Lewis calls it, that includes, in addition to a mass of factual data, many vividly rendered scenes of life both observed and imagined, concluding with a section called "The Meaning of All This" in which Du Bois lays out "the duty of the Negroes" and "the duty of the whites," and ending with a generous distribution of moral opinions on virtually everyone in sight (Lewis, *W. E. B. Du Bois*, 1:210). And this in a book that begins with a nervously personal confession in which Du Bois says that the scrupulous researcher "must ever tremble lest some personal bias, some moral conviction or some unconscious trend of thought due to previous training, has to a degree distorted the picture in his view" (*Philadelphia Negro*, 2)!

Du Bois's work does not, then, simply exemplify two kinds of mistakes a scholar can make; rather, it displays with hyper-real clarity the opposing energies and assumptions inherent, but generally neutralized or moderated, in all scholarship. In Du Bois we see both extremes of a debate that has defined modern scholarship between those who stress some concept of objectivity—the truth is found, not made, and rigorous method can neutralize subjective impurities—and those who emphasize the perspectival, literary, judgmental character of what is after all a human effort to understand human activity.

This debate suddenly emerged into the foreground of the field of history in the 1970s, when the historian Hayden White began to argue for the generic, narrative, literary, and generally imaginative character of the writing of history.[44] To many, it seemed that White was insisting that the discipline must change its fundamental self-understanding, abandoning any commitment to objectivism in favor of a dubiously postmodern understanding of the fictionality of all history. The reaction among conservative historians who thought that White represented the ignominious surrender of scholarship to fiction (and History to English) was sharp and swift. Sides were drawn, with each side declaring the other foolish and dangerous. But as becomes clear in Peter Novick's long and dizzying account of the entire debate, there was in fact no bright line between the two positions because even in the heat of battle each side was careful to make crucial concessions to the other. The objectivists acknowledged that of course history is not *all* grunt work and archival drudgery, that imagination and

41

judgment are also involved, while the relativists assured their nervous colleagues that they certainly did *not* mean to promote fantasy or invention at the expense of research.[45]

Du Bois himself did not linger in consideration of the complexities of the issue. Shortly after *The Philadelphia Negro* was published in early 1899, he was badly shaken by news of the lynching of a black man, Sam Hose, who had been accused of murder. He suddenly realized, as he said later, that he had "overworked a theory—that the cause of the problem was the ignorance of the people." He saw now that "the cure wasn't simply telling people the truth, it was inducing them to act on the truth."[46] He effectively left the world of scholarship and committed himself to a prodigiously active public life, writing for popular magazines, attending conferences, engaging in high-profile controversies, and organizing. He helped to found the Niagara Movement in 1905, which in turn led to the founding of the National Association for the Advancement of Colored People in 1909. And in 1910 he left Atlanta University to edit *The Crisis* for the NAACP, a position he held until 1934, when he rejoined the faculty at Atlanta University. Returning to university life after this long hiatus, he also returned to scholarship, publishing a six-hundred-page study, *Black Reconstruction in America,* in the following year.[47]

He had returned with a vengeance. Documenting the real contributions that black people made to civil society during Reconstruction, *Black Reconstruction in America* sought to disprove the commonly held belief that black people were incapable of participating in a democracy because they were inherently unintelligent, irresponsible, lazy, dishonest, and imprudent. There is, Du Bois acknowledges, much blame for the failure of Reconstruction to distribute, and in this instance, he betrays no sign of trembling at the thought that some personal moral conviction might infiltrate the work and delegitimate his judgments. But the real weight of Du Bois's disapprobation falls not on Southern revanchists but on the professional historians who gave racist arguments the patina of scholarship. These imposter scholars had attacked Reconstruction as a doomed attempt to integrate an unworthy black population, praised the Black Codes as reasonable and temperate, sought to rehabilitate the reputation of Andrew Johnson, and urged that the unfortunate sufferings of the past be forgotten in the interest of amity.

Du Bois rejects the proffered hand of friendship. In a final chapter, "The Propaganda of History," he accuses his fellow historians of a vile but commonplace scurrility, perpetrating falsehoods about Negro character and capacities by ignoring through a combination of sloth and willful ignorance all the evidence Du Bois had turned up in government records, organizational archives, and volumes of personal papers. "The whole history of Reconstruction," Du Bois writes, "has with few exceptions been written by passionate believers in the inferiority of the Negro," with the result that "I write . . . in a field devastated by passion and belief" (*Black Reconstruction*, 313, 593). He then names the malefactors—John W. Burgess, Walter Lynwood Fleming, Thomas Staples, and, above all, William A. Dunning—and the universities that employed them—Columbia, the University of North Carolina, the University of Virginia, Johns Hopkins University. And he points out that the evil done by these men and their supporting institutions extended well beyond the academy. In an extraordinary passage at the very end of his book, Du Bois conjures up the ultimate consequences of their scholarly malfeasance: "Immediately in Africa, a black back runs red with the blood of the lash; in India, a brown girl is raped; in China, a coolie starves; in Alabama, seven darkies are more than lynched; while in London, the white limbs of a prostitute are hung with jewels and silk. Flames of jealous murder sweep the earth, while brains of little children smear the hills" (596). Aware that he himself might be accused of passion and belief, Du Bois undertakes a rapid self-scrutiny. He finds nothing problematic. "I want," he says,

> to be fair, objective and judicial; to let no searing of the memory by intolerable insult and cruelty make me fail to sympathize with human frailties and contradiction. . . . But armed and warned by all this, and fortified by long study of the facts, I stand at the end of this writing, literally aghast at what American historians have done to this field. . . . I cannot believe that any unbiased mind, with an ideal of truth and of scientific judgment, can read the plain, authentic facts of our history, during 1860–1880, and come to conclusions essentially different from mine; and yet I stand virtually alone in this interpretation. (593–94)

In the long and bloody history of *odium scholasticum*, has any scholar ever been so utterly and openly contemptuous of *all* his colleagues?

In Du Bois's account, his fellow scholars had abused the office of scholarship. They had, through training and employment, been granted access to the relevant facts; but rather than taking a scholar's distance from prevailing views, rather than making a good-faith effort to neutralize personal biases, moral convictions, or unconscious trains of thought, they had voluntarily replicated social norms—indeed, they had provided erudite support for the worst and least normative of those norms. They had used the armature of scholarship to dignify their own wretched opinions. They had, perhaps deliberately, been derelict in the execution of their researcher's responsibilities to discover how it actually was. And they had adopted, without having earned, the rhetorical mode of scholarly authority, to the corruption of scholarship and, since scholarship has implications beyond itself, of the nation and even the world. Bone of the bone with the national racist consensus, they had *failed to be problematic*.

With respect to the discipline of scholarship, their offense was that they had failed not just to be persuaded by the facts but to be persuadable at all. They had resisted or denied the force of the evidence, and had even gone to some lengths to avoid confronting it. As I will argue at greater length in chapter 2, persuadability, or as I will put it there, convertibility is the core virtue of the scholar. A willingness to accord serious and fair-minded consideration even to possibilities that offend cherished values and beliefs, and to change one's mind if the evidence warrants it, is the signature of scholarly neutrality and, in a deeper sense, of human freedom. The honest scholar models freedom in holding his views open to the possibility of disconfirmation; the dishonest scholar who refuses to submit his thinking to a fresh field of evidence is a model not just of passion and belief but of reaction and dogma.

Du Bois himself did not always pass the persuadability test. Late in life, he was particularly intractable when it came to Communist leaders. He begins his *Autobiography* not with his birth or family history but with an account of his 1958 trip abroad, his first since 1951, when his passport had been confiscated because of his unwillingness to sign a statement saying he was not a member of the Communist Party. In fact, while not an official Party member, he was a committed Communist, a fact easily inferred from many documents, including a reverential essay he wrote on the death of Stalin.[48] In the *Autobiography*, he records his support for the Soviet suppression of the Hungarian uprising, which had, in his view, been led by "pushing businessmen and artisans" (13). Traveling around Eastern Europe, he becomes entirely convinced that "the majority of intelligent people . . . quite evidently . . . want communism" (13). And why not, when the Communist government of the Soviet Union, having abolished exploitation, is now hard at work "making new people, a disciplined people" (19)? In recognition of his long history of support for communism, Du Bois is made a member of the Hungarian Academy, receives an honorary degree from Lomonosov State University in Moscow, and is granted a private audience with Prime Minister Khrushchev, who gives him the Lenin Prize. In China, he dines with Mao Tse-Tung and Zhou Enlai. He is given a tour, on which he observes that the Chinese people are becoming freer, abandoning ranks and classes, and even doing away with invidious sex distinctions. With "leaders of skill and genius, scientists of renown, artisans of skill and millions who know and believe this and follow where these men lead," the Chinese nation, Du Bois says, now constitutes a "vast and glorious . . . miracle" (30, 31).

These are, of course, political positions rather than scholarly judgments. They are considered and deliberate judgments nevertheless, and evidence that might have contradicted or complicated them was not hard to find. But the point is not that the elderly Du Bois had lost a step, or that his intellectual joints had stiffened. Opinions that seem wrong to the majority, or wrong to a subsequent generation, are bone of the bone with those that seem right, now or later. The difference between informed opinion and mere opinion is not always visible on the surface. Because of the kind and amount of the labor that preceded them, scholarly opinions or judgments are often quite unyielding and ungenerous to alternatives. Scholarship is assertion, and self-assertion. All scholars must at least imply if they do not, like Du Bois, state outright their judgment that previous scholars have produced values masquerading as facts, that they have been misled by prejudice or sloth or poor judgment, or that good intentions notwithstanding, they have for some reason seen only part of the picture. The implicit message of all scholarship is *"X has been misunderstood until now."* Every scholarly work represents itself not just as the very best the author could do but as the best that could be done. And so, also implicit in every scholarly work is the conviction given defiant voice by Du Bois: *"I cannot believe that any unbiased mind could come to conclusions different from mine."*

This belief typically remains implicit because it conflicts with the other premise of scholarship, that scholarly conclusions represent not incontrovertible facts but individual judgments, and no virtuoso has a special or privileged relation to the truth. The judgment of the scholarly community is always dispositive, and every scholar must acknowledge that in the fullness of time, his work will be proven by his successors to be inadequate, misguided, dead wrong, or even wicked. The ritual statement in the acknowledgments page of scholarly works to the effect that all the brilliant things in this book belong to others, while the blunders that remain are the author's alone, testifies to this premise. The most gifted and assiduous scholar must embrace his own supercession.

One can go wrong by overestimating one's virtuosity; one always goes wrong by overstating it. But virtuosity is fully half of a scholar's virtue; the transformation of a mass of inert, confusing, and unsorted data into the truth of things is a deeply personal act requiring discipline, judiciousness, and a certain courage. The scholar ever feels his two-ness as he struggles to synthesize the rule-bound and impersonal activity of aggregating and accurately representing the evidence and the freer, more intuitive, and riskier processes of analyzing, interpreting, organizing, and representing the truth to which the evidence, in his view, bears witness.

CHAPTER TWO

Conversion and the Question of Evidence

A HANDSOME YOUNG MAN, having come of age in a warm and loving family in a strong and supportive community in a nation with a proud history, attends the prestigious university in his home town. A committed Christian, he decides early on to become a professor in New Testament studies and begins years of training, studying languages, philology, history, philosophy, and theology. He believes that a scholarly understanding of the Bible can provide ways of reconciling the demands of a traditional faith with the needs of the modern world. He considers that since religious faith is a powerful unifying force within his community, Biblical scholarship will not only provide him with a career, but will also benefit others. His future is predictably quiet, clear, and bright; he looks forward to a life of faith, study, and service.

For graduate school, he travels far from home, attending a prominent European university, where his teachers, impressed by his talent and commitment, encourage him. He undertakes a study of St. Paul's Epistles, including the Letter to the Galatians, an important and problematic text that offers challenges pertinent to today's culture, in which faith is so sorely tested. He is deeply alarmed by some features of the European academy. At the dissertation defense of a fellow student, the professor says, "Sir, you have written six hundred pages and still we know nothing about the subject"; to which the student replies, "That can only be because you have understood nothing I have written." And the student passes! And they share a drink after!

Not all of his experiences with free speech turn out so well. He is disturbed to find that some of his ideas, unquestioned at home, are not widely shared here, and are even regarded as morally flawed. He often finds himself outnumbered, on the losing end of debates. This makes him angry and defensive, especially when the debate migrates from Biblical hermeneutics to ethical principles and social policy. Even history, which he had regarded as a factual field, seems open for discussion. Is nothing sacred? After four years, degree achieved, he returns home and begins his career in earnest.

He continues his work on Paul's Letter to the Galatians. The text is endlessly fascinating, and he is on the front lines of discovery. He is becoming known as one of the most promising young scholars in his field. The larger community takes notice as well, because this field is widely understood to be a source of theological support for ideas circulating throughout society, ideas that the national and local governments regard as central to their legitimacy, and to the idea of the nation itself.

For many years, the community to which the young scholar belonged had seen itself as a modern version of the embattled early Christian church, persecuted by its enemies but strengthened by its faith. As those early Christians had survived and triumphed, so would the community of today. The evidence of God's approval was not only inscribed in the Bible; it could be seen in history itself. The path to freedom had been long and harsh, and even today circumstances remained challenging. But surely, people felt, divine Providence had played a role in sustaining the community through difficult days in the past, and would continue to do so in the future if the community remained faithful.

In this context, one of the most valuable civic functions a Biblical scholar could perform was to clarify and thereby strengthen the resemblance of the situation faced by the early Christians to the one faced by believers in the modern world. Paul's Epistles, and in particular his Letter to the Galatians, with its strong words against those who would stray from or pervert the faith, would be crucial to the nation's self-understanding. The nation has much to learn from Paul, who rallies the Galatians by telling them that the faithful are "called unto liberty." "Stand fast," Paul writes, "in the liberty with which Christ hath made us free" (Gal. 5:13, Gal. 5:1). The full emancipatory potentiality of Paul's message in the contemporary world is waiting to be unfurled; the Letter requires inspired explication, which our young man feels he can provide.

And yet, disturbed by the memory of those student discussions in which he had fared so poorly, he struggles to formulate better responses than he had been able to command at the time. He turns, naturally, to Paul's Letter for guidance. But what's this? On examination, key distinctions seem weaker and more complicated than he had remembered. He finds himself bewildered and almost irritated by a key passage in which Paul describes a Christian community defined not by identity but by common belief, a community in which "there is neither Jew nor Greek" (Gal. 3:28). Faith is supremely important, but why claim that it effaces natural differences? What is a community if it comprises, higgledy-piggledy, anyone and everyone who decides one day to have faith—if you can join it or leave it just by changing your mind?

The continuation of 3:28 makes things worse for anyone seeking clarity: "there is neither Jew nor Greek, there is neither slave nor free, there is neither male nor female; for you are all one in Christ Jesus." These words were apparently intended to inspire a feeling of oceanic oneness, but what a mess! Another passage troubles him for a different reason. Paul reminds the Galatians of their faithless past, when they "did service unto them which by nature are no gods" (Gal. 4:8). Can only gods rule? (And why the plural?) And what's wrong with service, which has characterized human societies from the beginning of time? There is a natural, God-created order of things—nations, sexes, races, classes, categories of all kinds, some higher, some lower—and to love God is to respect His pluriform creation. Is it not?

He is vexed. If the text that he believed supported his world in fact supports another, entirely different world, a world he cannot recognize or find a home in, then what's the world coming to? There must be a way out of this. He returns to the text.

Our gifted young man has come upon an unexpected crisis of faith—not faith in God, which remains for him unshaken, but faith in evidence. What does the text actually say? The entire drama seems to center on the question of the evidence; or rather, it seems to lead into the cave of a deeper question: What is evidence?

In one sense, the question is easily answered. Information about the human past is provided by many things, but the richest sources are documents. Ranke particularly prized what he called "genuine and original documents," especially "the narratives of eye-witnesses," which could, he said, provide immediate, direct transcriptions of experience.[1] A genuine and original document had, Ranke felt, the incomparable advantage of proximity to the thing it described or recorded. As a first transcription of reality, such documents retained a certain innocence uncorrupted by any deforming agenda or presupposition that might arise in years to come as imperfect scholars perhaps unwittingly sought confirmation in the historical record for their own views.

Documents have two further advantages for the scholar. First, they exist in material form, even if the things they refer to do not or do no longer; and second, they are textual, and so available for direct incorporation into the work of scholarship in a way that centuries, wars, nations, economies, ideologies, cathedrals, patterns, and individuals are not. And so, while Ranke has been much criticized, and his credulity toward eyewitness accounts questioned and even ridiculed, the privilege of documents remains as a fundamental principle of scholarship because documents are singularly well suited to providing what scholars need: evidence.

But as Lionel Gossman says, "We do not well understand the relation between evidence and the theories or narratives it is used to sustain or refute" (*Between History and Literature,* 320). Why should this be a problem? If arguments require the evidence that documents provide, where is the confusion? The culprit is the documentary nature of evidence itself. On the one hand, documents provide the scholar with an objective foundation or ground for his argument. Everything else in a scholar's work may be questioned or disputed, but the documents on which the work is based cannot: these actually exist, they are the rock beneath the sand, and any argument must somehow be based on them. But they do not explain themselves. They can be hard to find, tedious to absorb, difficult to organize, and incomplete or misleading in the picture they provide. If the document is genuine and original in Ranke's sense, then the owl of Minerva had not yet flown when it was produced, so even the most conscientiously prepared document can only provide evidence not of how it really was but merely of what it, or a fragment of it, may have seemed like to one small person at one fleeting moment.

Then, too, scholarship involves not just discovery or reproduction but also analysis and interpretation, human processes involving judgment and, almost inevitably, error. And compelling though they may be, documents are inherently incomplete, partial, and preliminary. They can lead a well-intentioned but impatient scholar to wander off into a fogbank of theory, to formulate through fatigue or overconfidence premature generalizations, to impose a narrative form on events that exhibited no such form when they were happening, or to pronounce with a satisfying finality on the meaning of it all. Theory, generalization, form—these are all honorable and necessary scholarly functions, but they involve a risky separation from the evidence. If a disconnect between argument and evidence becomes apparent, the argument wobbles, and the scholar may be admonished by his peers to return to the true path of scholarship by undertaking some form of a "return to philology," a refocusing on the ontology of the document, a rebaptism in the primal waters of empiricism. But such a return might not solve the problem: philology was at once the most hyper-empirical and the most flagrantly—indeed disastrously—speculative of all research programs.[2]

So, in response to the original question, we can say that evidence is what is provided by documents. The inescapable question is now whether documents can hold up under the weight they are asked to bear.

To anyone other than a scribe, a typesetter, or a paleographer, documents command attention because of their content, which is perhaps a misnomer because documents do not contain their content. Rather, they represent it. Documents are cited in scholarly works as evidence on the premise that the real evidence that the documents record or refer to cannot speak for itself. The seed does not declare the flower, which must be inferred from it. This "real evidence" must be considered potential evidence until it takes documentary form, at which point the document itself becomes the evidence, although the only thing it truly proves is that something has been converted into documentary form.

Documents are, then, not only the indispensable form of evidence but also incontrovertible evidence of their own insufficiency and unreliability as evidence. Evidence is at best "good enough," without being perfect. And since everything represented in a document has been translated out of itself in the course of assuming documentary form, every document can be questioned for the accuracy of its translation. Embedded within the evidence are a host of invisible alternatives, choices, and roads not taken. A scholarly argument represents a variable inference from the documentary evidence, which itself represents an inference from the real evidence. A principle of freedom is secreted in the law. The gaps between the real evidence and the document, and between the document and the argument, can only be overcome through a leap of faith. It is the task of the scholar to make that leap seem as short and safe as possible, and to persuade his readers that it was no leap at all, really, just a simple and almost inevitable step. But there is a gap, and there was a leap.

A further complicating factor is the material document itself, which, once produced, begins a career that might include copying, translation, editing, forgery, redaction, reproduction, publication, and dissemination just in order to exist in the present. Then, the final complication: everything leading to the production of the document anticipates a reader who will understand it; but the reader, who is perhaps sitting in a library carrel thousands of miles and centuries removed from the site of the document's production, is faced with the daunting task of peering back in time through the document to the thing being represented or expressed, which, as previously noted, may have been misperceived, misunderstood, poorly rendered, misrepresented, or even falsified: one of the earliest instances of evidence-based "modern" scholarship is Lorenzo Valla's 1440 philological exposé of the "Donation of Constantine," the forged document that supposedly gave the Pope authority over the Western Roman Empire.[3] At the very beginning, scholarship was devoted to subtracting rather than adding to the sum of knowledge; or rather, we might say that its addition consisted of a subtraction.

In short, scholarship constantly seeks a documentary origin as the rock on which the church of understanding must be built; but, just as relentlessly, it reveals the rock already to be a church, sustained by faith, which may or may not be founded on a rock.

It would seem, then, that even, or perhaps especially, genuine and original documents require more evidence in order for anyone to arrive at a proper understanding of them. Even documents require documentation. The art historian Erwin Panofsky approaches this paradox from another direction in a famous 1939 essay, "The History of Art as a Humanistic Discipline," in which he distinguishes between the natural sciences and the humanities on the basis that the latter deal with *"the records left by man."*[4] Panofsky identifies two kinds of records, documents and monuments. Documents provide evidence in the form of information or perspective about monuments that the monuments cannot provide by themselves, as a contract might provide evidence about an altar. The distinction between the two seems clear enough, but as Panofsky notes, both are products of human agency and so have a family resemblance. One is not conceptual or ideal and the other mutely material: thoughts have real impact on human lives, and everything humans make bears meaning and value only insofar as it registers the force and form of concepts. Documents and monuments exist therefore in a "hopeless vicious circle": not only are the documents just as enigmatic as the monuments themselves, but at any moment a shift of perspective can convert one into the other, so that "everyone's 'monuments' are everyone else's 'documents,' and vice versa" (10).[5]

One implication of this bewildering formulation is that knowledge is volitional. Every document reflects a decision to treat something as a document. The knowledge produced by scholarship is therefore to an uncertain degree constructed by the scholar or by previous scholars. As I said at the end of chapter 1, the scholar is personally accountable for his conclusions in a way that the scientist, for example, is not.[6] This fact may weaken the claim of scholarship to scientific certitude, or what is imagined to be scientific certitude, but it also has the compensatory advantage of liberating the scholar from subservience to brute fact. Because it is found in documents, the evidence with which scholars work does not function for the scholar like a machine, an algorithm, God, or Reason; evidence is rather dispositive, a strong recommendation with some freedom of judgment or interpretation assumed.

The volitional character of scholarly evidence was almost a founding recognition in many scholarly fields. In his widely influential 1961 book *What Is History?*,[7] E. H. Carr beats the dead horse of the "cult of facts" in the discipline of history mercilessly, giving a brutally brief history of what he considers a deluded but mysteriously compelling belief attributable to the influence of Ranke, followed by a more leisurely and admiring chronicle of defections from the cult by Wilhelm Dilthey, Benedetto Croce, Carl Becker, R. G. Collingwood, and Michael Oakeshott. All these, in Carr's account, contributed elements of what has become an overwhelming consensus that facts do not exist independent of the historian's interpretation, do not speak for themselves, are never available for a neutral or nonsubjective inspection—in short, that "history is what the historian makes" (29).

So thorough, dismissive, and assured is the drubbing given to poor Ranke (b. 1795) that one wonders why Carr thought him worth repudiating at all. One reason may be that while history, like other scholarly disciplines, cannot conduct its business as a cult of facts, neither can it simply renounce all aspirations to the factual truth and give itself over to a cult of fiction or fantasy. Paul Valéry's assertion that history is "a piece of imagination based on records"[8] is not inaccurate, but the statement is too blunt and unequivocal, gliding too rapidly over the delicate question implied by "based on." Scholarship must continually balance the claims of two opposing cults, producing arguments that claim to represent how it really was while conceding, at least in theory, the role of evaluations, interpretations, selections, and decisions in the formulation of that truth and even in the constitution of the evidence. Thinking, perhaps, of the unstable dialectic at the core of his discipline, Carr may have invoked Ranke's name with the double purpose of recalling the discipline's founding commitment to the concept of fact and warning against an extreme version of that commitment.

To the scholar, documents are objects invested with a kind of value that excites interest. Indeed, one striking feature of scholars' discourse about scholarship is the affective richness of the metaphors that even meticulous scholars use to describe their materials. The historian Hugh Trevor-Roper has written that "a historian ought to love the past: that is the test of his vocation."[9] Trevor-Roper is probably not saying that scholars ought to form passionate personal commitments to their materials, but he may be saying, perhaps without intending to, that scholars invest their materials with their own ideas, desires, hopes, needs, and interests, and yet still manage to persuade themselves that they love those materials for themselves alone. He would undoubtedly approve of the historian Peter Brown, who studies the monastic communities and solitary desert ascetics that arose in Late Antiquity. To modern eyes, early Christian asceticism can appear as a kind of death cult predicated on theological mania, misanthropy, misogyny, shame, self-denial, sexual panic, and body-hatred, but Brown, like Trevor-Roper, regards all this with the fond eye of the lover:

> To modern persons, whatever their religious beliefs, the Early Christian themes of sexual renunciation, of continence, celibacy, and the virgin life have come to carry with them icy overtones. . . . [Yet] even today, these notions still crowd in upon us, as pale, forbidding presences. Historians must bring to them their due measure of warm, red blood. By studying their precise social and religious context, the scholar can give back to these ideas a little of the human weight that they once carried in their own time. When such an offering is made, the chill shades may speak to us again, and perhaps more gently than we had thought they might, in the strange tongue of a long-lost Christianity.[10]

With this image of long-dead desert eremites whispering tendresses in the historian's ear, Brown makes vividly explicit the "loving" attitude of the scholar as he applies to documentary traces of long-dead fanaticisms the vivifying touch of erudition, discipline, and sympathy.

Brown's strangely impressive effusion might be considered a half-humorous attempt to engage the reader by depicting the scholar, surrounded by books in a quiet room, in an agitated state. But what are we to make of the startling Dantesque opening to Stephen Greenblatt's *Shakespearean Negotiations,* which, like Brown's passage, invokes the vitality and volubility of the long-deceased: "I began with the desire to speak with the dead"?[11] This desire, which Greenblatt describes as "a familiar, if unvoiced, motive in literary studies," might also be considered an attempt to warm up the image of the scholar in the eyes of the reader, even at the expense of the scholar's dignity. But Greenblatt pursues his metaphor, describing documents from the past as "fragment[s] of lost life" that somehow contain human presences patiently but eagerly awaiting the scholar's arrival (1).

Why is desire rather than, say, curiosity so consistently invoked in accounts of scholarship? Perhaps the answer is that curiosity represents a drier, more dispassionate kind of interest that can be satisfied when the solution to the problem is found, whereas desire suggests a yearning without end or limit. This factor of infinity aligns with the nature of the document as Greenblatt understands it. Texts, he argues, are misconstrued as expressions of a single mind directed at the mind of the reader. In fact, the text is but a node in an "astonishingly open" process of "structured negotiation and exchange" that he calls "social energy" (*Shakespearean Negotiations,* 19, 6). His descriptions of social energy typically take the form of lists that seem like they could go on forever: "a subtle, elusive set of exchanges, a network of trades and trade-offs, a jostling of competing representations, a negotiation between competing joint-stock companies" engaged in ceaseless movements of interpenetration and transformation across shifting and permeable boundaries (7). Nothing in the arena of social energy is wholly, solely, or permanently itself, everything is available for transformation and circulation, everything is open to everything else. The only fixed point—and that not fixed at all—is the text, the site of all these negotiations, exchanges, and circulations.[12]

To scholars discouraged by the tedium of working with obdurately inert and withholding materials, the prospect of all that seething life, worlds swirling within worlds, might seem a thrilling liberation. But there is a reason why the desire to speak with the dead is "often unvoiced." If evidence was seen as alive and attractive, and the scholar as eagerly desiring, then the distance required for knowledge would vanish, and the scholar would be writing love letters rather than scholarship. Nothing if not bold, however, Greenblatt doubles down on his metaphor: "Even when I came to understand that in my most intense moments of straining to listen [to the dead] all I could hear was my own voice, even then I did not abandon my desire. It was true that I could hear only my own voice, but my own voice was the voice of the dead" (1). A compelling vignette with which to begin a book, this necro-fantasy yet carries great risk, for by claiming to speak not only with the dead but for them and even as them, Greenblatt has confessed to a corrupting desire that takes him out of the domain of scholarship altogether.

How does the scholar preserve the idea of truth while still acknowledging that scholarship is a human activity animated by human interests? There is a way, and Greenblatt discovers it. In his opening pages he describes how he began with an initial hypothesis in which Shakespeare's plays "precipitated out of a sublime confrontation between a total artist and a totalizing society. . . . The result of this confrontation between total artist and totalizing society was a set of unique, inexhaustible, and supremely powerful works of art" (2). Greenblatt is asking his reader to believe that his original conception was submitted to the test of a fresh reading of Shakespeare's plays, and—to Greenblatt's surprise—it did not survive. The conception buckled because the text failed to provide evidence for the conclusions he had wanted to draw. Bereft of his premises, Greenblatt is then forced to read with if not an innocent at least a nervously disoriented eye. Doing so, he discovers unsuspected evidence not of totalization but of . . . social energy. *Shakespearean Negotiations* is, he says, the result of his awakening to this new understanding. "In the book," Greenblatt explains, "something of this original conception survives, but it has been complicated by several turns in my thinking that I had not foreseen. I can summarize those turns by remarking that I came to have doubts about two things: 'total artist' and 'totalizing society'" (2).

It is difficult to believe that the famously au courant Greenblatt really began with the belief in a sublime confrontation between a totalizing artist and a totalizing society, or with a neo-Romantic confidence that he could achieve an unmediated intimacy with the text when such concepts had been authoritatively debunked for many years. In his famous 1917 lecture "Science as a Vocation," Max Weber argued that there were strict limits on the kinds of problems scholarship, or "science," could address, and condemned such concepts as sublimity, immediacy, and totalization as forms of Romantic or quasi-theological irrationalism that lay beyond the pale of any inquiry that claimed validity.[13] Opposition to this view is today hard to find—so why does Greenblatt ask his reader to believe that he began with notions already long discredited?

The reason may be that, having placed his stature and even his professional identity as a scholar in jeopardy by indulging in seductive rhetorical gambits, he then seeks to reassure the reader that it was not his voice after all—that he was not actually in love with the dead, not exchanging soft words with the dead, not speaking for the dead, and not himself dead, but was rather listening in a state of chastened attentiveness to the dead as they spoke their own truth. The form this reassurance takes is a small narrative of defeat in which the proud, confident, and warm-blooded scholar approaches the text in a state of hopeful expectation only to be rebuked for his presumption and instructed to think otherwise. Unimpressed by the scholar's approach, the evidence exercises force majeure, insisting on its own prerogatives and compelling him, against his will and even at some cost to his self-esteem, to renounce his cherished convictions, unquestioned assumptions, and even what he had taken as common sense, and humble himself before the truth. Scholarship begins in humility, and even in humiliation.

Such a narrative may be embarrassing to the scholar as a male, but it reflects well on his commitment to the vocation of scholarship, for it demonstrates that he has exercised the right kind of freedom, voluntarily performing an act of self-dissociation so that he can confront the evidence honestly. He has also, according to this narrative, denied himself the pleasures of the wrong kinds of freedom, the freedom to interfere with or impose himself on the evidence and bend it to his will, or to see it through the filter of his own unchecked or unacknowledged desires or preconceptions. Of course, the scholar may be making up the scenario itself, or may be uncertain whether he is making it up; he may not actually know whether he has found or created the evidence by which he claims to be compelled.[14] But in his role as a scholar he is compelled to believe that he has discovered the truth.

Not every work of scholarship contains *petits récits* of pride brought low, but all works imply an experience in which the scholar comes to the subject with a hypothesis—how else could one approach it?—that is disconfirmed in some way by the evidence, forcing the scholar to convert from what he was to what he ought to be, or, to put it another way, to renounce his ideas about what he feels the truth ought to be and embrace the truth as it actually is. In the discipline of scholarship, preconceptions or assumptions are always suspect because they have not been freshly hammered out on the anvil of evidence. The mark of the scholar, and the core of the scholarly ethic, is this willingness to return to the forge and to beat, and be beaten, anew.

So central to scholarship is this drama of renunciation and awakening that some scholars, including perhaps Greenblatt in this instance, are actually eager to construct a story in which their foolishness, naïveté, pride, or confusion is exposed by an honest confrontation with resistant evidence. The real interest of the story and the source of its power have, however, nothing to do with the individual scholar. The narrative confers authority on the scholar and his work because it represents the fundamental structure of scholarship. As an orderly and progressive activity, scholarship values continuity. It cannot extend the hand of welcome to any crackpot theory or wild interpretation that presents itself. But if scholarship becomes too effective in policing the field, it risks closing off the kind of innovation and challenges to received views that are not just essential sources of renewal but its only raison d'être. Degenerating into mythology or dogma, scholarship could become its own worst enemy, the greatest threat to its own freedom and to freedom in general. Prizing continuity, however, scholarship must also value transformation, welcoming change as long as it occurs for the right reasons, under the right constraints. An individual who demonstrates, perhaps by a small and homely narrative that at first seems to reflect poorly on him, that he respects precedent by approaching a problem with preconceptions formed by previous scholarship and by his own habit of congeniality, but then renounces those preconceptions in obedience to the evidence and produces something new, honors the discipline in a way consistent with its basic premises.[15]

One might wish that one could defend scholarship as a discourse of truth by saying that every scholarly work involves a conversion experience in which the scholar submits to the overmastering force of the evidence, his resistance broken on the wheel of fact. But scholarship can make no such claim. Painful though it is to say so, we must acknowledge that evidence is also something a scholar does to himself—even, if some are to be believed, something that he loves doing to himself.

Now we may return to our learned young man, wrestling with difficulties he never expected to encounter. In fact, we may permit that half-fictionalized and imagined figure to assume the aspect of a real person: Bernard C. Lategan, born into an Afrikaner family in 1938 and baptized the day of a public event that catalyzed an immense surge of Afrikaner nationalism, the one-hundredth anniversary of the Great Trek, the heroic migration of Afrikaners northward in the middle of the nineteenth century to escape British rule in the Cape Colony.

The son of a man deeply committed to the cause of Afrikaner identity and the Afrikaans language as the expression of that identity, Lategan grew up steeped in the mythology of the Afrikaner people. At the root of this mythology were concepts of freedom and democracy, as well as religious faith, as taught by the Dutch Reformed Church (DRC), the dominant church in the country. The

FIGURE 2. Bernard Lategan, 2012, *photo Robert Letz.*

reenactment of the Great Trek was staged as an affirmation of a powerful identification of the Afrikaner people and the Israelites who escaped from slavery in Egypt to the promised land. In his youth, Lategan was a founding member of the Ruiterwag, a secret youth organization that served as a recruiting arm of the semisecret Broederbond (Brotherhood), which had been formed in the 1920s in order to protect the interests of the Afrikaners, then a marginalized and impotent group. After the victory of the National Party in the general election of 1948, Afrikaners acquired political power, and the Broederbond became a powerful instrument to consolidate the new position, whose distinctive expression was the system of apartheid. With the assistance of the Broederbond, Afrikaner ideology assumed a totalizing control not just over politics, language, and religion but over social life at all levels, exerting influence over where one banked, which clubs one belonged to, which books one read, who one's friends were, one's career prospects. No matter where one turned—to the government, the Church, the professions, the army, the press, the educational institutions—power was held by those committed to the Afrikaner ideology. In time, Lategan joined the Broederbond.

He attended Stellenbosch University, one of the oldest universities in South Africa, which counted among its former students many government officials, including every South African prime minister between 1919 and 1978. The list includes Hendrik Verwoerd, who can be seen on video, smiling as he defines apartheid in 1961 as a policy of "good neighborliness."[16] For graduate school, Lategan went to the Netherlands, where he earned his doctoral degree in New Testament Studies, writing a dissertation on the earthly Jesus in Paul's preaching before returning to South Africa in 1967. After a brief ministry, he took a faculty position at the University of the Western Cape, a newly formed "Coloured" university (with an all-white faculty), intending to study the word of God in service to the Afrikaner people and the nation.

The role of academia in sustaining the apartheid system was to promulgate, through teaching, symposia, congresses, and published research, a version of history that explained and justified the system, a version that an intelligent and conscientious person could believe. The role of the Church was to develop theological justifications for this history.[17] Among the religious—a group that encompassed virtually everyone of importance in Afrikaner society[18]—it was widely accepted that the Bible provided unimpeachable evidence for the righteousness of the Afrikaner cause. Biblical scholarship had a special responsibility to identify and disseminate this evidence because, in a widely held view, the real basis of apartheid was the Church's mission policy, based on principles of "sphere sovereignty" and "separate development" that were themselves based on respect for the God-created diversity of the human race, as evidenced in the Bible.

Unlike forms of racism or xenophobia in other countries, apartheid was understood by its proponents as an ideology of freedom for all—for Afrikaners now and for others in due time and within certain limits. It was also based on religious devotion. In the view of the Church, the Bible was authoritative and luminously clear as a guide to political practice, particularly so on the issue of racial segregation. As one scholar said, the prevailing view in the Dutch Reformed Church held that "the mother of all questions is the question of race relations and that the mother of all books, the Bible, speaks with authority on issues of Babel."[19] In this interpretation, apartheid was not only the law of the land; it was the law of God.

Under the circumstances, one of the most valuable tasks a scholar could perform was to locate in the Bible accounts of the origins of human diversity. The obvious candidate, the Babel story in Genesis, was interpreted as God's punishment for the attempt to establish a unitary order in defiance of the multiplicity of Creation. To objections that the

Genesis account actually argued for the aboriginal unity of humankind, Afrikaner Biblical scholars replied that the diversity of the physical world was the real point of origin, and the situation following the punishment after Babel was simply the restoration of an ontological diversity present at the creation. To each his own: one eminent scholar, W. Nicol, assured his readers in 1947 that "whites could be good Christians, and at the same time watch over the survival of their race with holy gravity."[20] Paul's Letter to the Galatians could be interpreted in this spirit as well, as an account of a spiritual community united in Christ but separate and distinct from other communities. The Church honored the principle of multiplicity in its own structure by establishing four separate churches, for whites (the "mother" church), blacks, Indians, and Coloureds. In his early writings, Lategan described the community of Christ as an "invisible" community that accepts existing diversity but anticipates a fuller realization when this sinful world will be replaced at the Second Coming.[21]

Apartheid ideology, as is already apparent, was insistently archeological, explaining present conditions by reference to their (Biblical) origins.[22] Afrikaner theologians, and Afrikaner people generally, saw themselves and their reality depicted in the Bible with a compelling directness, discovering in it a heroic account of their own struggles, their own faith, their own mission. The Bible was their inspiration as they wrested their freedom from the British, and again as they created a new democratic nation founded on principles of generosity, respect, and freedom. The Word of God was their own myth, but it was not mere myth, because sophisticated Biblical scholarship had established a sound historical basis and modern interpretive strategies for understanding its message.

It is, and has long been, tempting for a secular citizen of a European or North American country to regard all this as a particular evil—a "separate development" perhaps—arising in the singularly depraved society of South Africa. Far from the enlightened societies of the West but claiming some distant kindred with them, set on a course of self-preservation in which strange and evil ways were miscast as divine revelation, devoted to racial self-interest in a way that advanced societies had long since repudiated, and cruelly insensitive to the facts of oppression that were self-evident to anyone not under the spell of the mass delusion that had seized the Afrikaner people, the South African nation had walled itself off in its own criminalized sphere. For many in the West, these were very attractive and useful thoughts.

But such thoughts overstate the differences. Popular movements of national liberation or self-assertion are invariably accompanied by, and in fact built upon, exclusion and violence. As Ernest Renan said in "What Is a Nation?" in 1882, nations have much to remember—the national myth of origin, each nation's own Great Trek—and much to forget, as, in the case of France, the St. Bartholomew's Day Massacre. The United States presents a number of particularly glaring examples of nation-founding omissions or forgettings, beginning with what Du Bois described as the fatal compromise struck in the Constitution between the federal government and the Southern colonies that permitted the continuance and, as it turned out, the immense expansion of slavery.[23]

Nor does the United States lack for those who would conscript religion in the hard labor of reaction. In the present day, many American religious leaders have supported, either explicitly or implicitly, policies, programs, and pronouncements that perpetuate and even expand the parameters of prejudice, extending beyond race to include religions, nations, political parties, and persons; and they have often cited the Bible as evidence for the justice of their support. To take just one recent instance, on 14 June 2018, U.S. Attorney General Jeff Sessions defended the Trump administration's policy of separating families of asylum-seekers at the southern border, and rebuked protesters by referring to Romans 13:1–2: "For there is no power but of God; the powers that be are ordained of God. Whosoever, therefore, resisteth the power, resisteth the ordinance of God."

Critics immediately noted that this verse had been widely cited by Southern religious leaders who claimed divine authority for slave laws in the antebellum South. And as it happens, this same useful verse had also figured prominently in the apologetics of theologians who supported apartheid.[24] But the DRC had abandoned the argument that God supported apartheid long before 2018. Condemned in the late 1970s by European Protestant churches for its support for apartheid, the DRC had undergone a long and contentious project of self-scrutiny that concluded in 1986 with a guarded repudiation of apartheid by the main branch of the Church, provoking a 1987 schismatic break in which some five thousand revanchist members of the DRC left to form their own Afrikaner branch. With respect to the citation of Biblical support for manifest injustice and discrimination, the main body of the Dutch Reformed Church was more advanced than some American Protestants.

In the field of Biblical hermeneutics, the salient South African difference was that issues being debated on North American college campuses as if they were strictly theoretical were, in South Africa, tangled up in a convulsive nationwide movement of radical social transformation. Among these issues was the question of evidence, the subject of a special issue of a leading journal of literary theory published in 1991 at the University of Chicago. In the introduction to the expanded volume that followed, the editors noted that evidence was an issue in many academic disciplines—"deconstruction, gender studies, New Historicism, cultural studies, new approaches to the history and philosophy of science, the critical legal studies movement, and so on."[25] And so on—but not in the streets.

In the South African context, by contrast, questions of evidence were among the most divisive and consequential issues in society, with controversies swirling around, for example, the dubious evidence presented by the government at the 1963 trial of Nelson Mandela and nine others for conspiracy and sabotage. The issues of freedom and compulsion raised by the question of evidence had in the South African context a brutal pertinence not always registered in Western academic discourse of the time, finely nuanced though it was. And yet, as we will see, the critical distance—and the nuances—provided by theory were crucial to Lategan's efforts to liberate the Bible from the embrace of the national government.

Since the context for the discussion of evidence was worldly rather than academic, we must sketch out, as efficiently as possible, a more detailed narrative of events in order to understand the nature of the critical and political issues Lategan and others were wrestling with. What follows is at best an abbreviated schematic rendering of a turbulent time, with endless meetings of overlapping groups, documents in various draft stages, and official statements in which scholars and Church officials sought to maintain some semblance of reasoned deliberation in an atmosphere of violence in which nobody's survival could be assured.[26]

Over the course of the 1970s, an increasingly chaotic and violent decade marked indelibly by the murderous suppression of the 1976 Soweto uprising, Lategan had grown increasingly disaffected from the apartheid regime and increasingly doubtful that any Biblical sanction for it could be honestly discovered. He was, at the same time, becoming impatient with the Dutch Reformed Church for failing to take the initiative in reassessing the role of religion in contemporary political affairs. Pressured by an inflamed domestic situation, the DRC at last began to move, declaring at the General Synod in 1978 that apartheid was a sin. This declaration was not enough for the Dutch Reformed Mission Church—the "Coloured" branch of the DRC. In 1982, three years after Lategan had left the University of the Western Cape to go to Stellenbosch University, the Dutch Reformed Mission Church issued a statement saying that they had no choice, "but with the deepest regret, to accuse the Dutch Reformed Church of theological heresy and idolatry in the light of the DRC theological formulated stance and the implementation thereof in practice."[27] In 1982, this group drafted a document that became known as the Belhar Confession, which condemned apartheid in far stronger terms than the DRC had been able to agree on.

Three years later, in 1985, the World Alliance of Reformed Churches suspended the DRC's membership on the grounds that the DRC had misused the gospel to justify apartheid. In the same year, a group of primarily black theologians based in Soweto challenged the state of emergency recently declared by the government by issuing the Kairos Document,[28] which rejected in the strongest terms the concept of "state theology," challenging in particular the official understanding of Romans 13:1–7 about the religious necessity of obedience to the worldly powers that be. The following year, the DRC, stunned and chastened by worldwide condemnation, published *Church and Society*, which announced the new official view of the Church, that "a forced separation and division of peoples cannot be considered a Biblical imperative. The attempt to justify such an injunction as derived from the Bible must be recognized as an error and rejected."[29]

Before this time, Lategan's gestures of resistance had been legible only to South African Biblical scholars who could divine in arguments about, for example, the correct reading of Acts 17:26, which speaks in suggestive but ambiguous terms of "the nations of men" and the divinely determined "bounds of their habitation," encrypted indications of opposition to the apartheid regime. He made a nearer approach to the literal and direct in an article published in 1984 with the almost assertively unexciting title "Current Issues in the Hermeneutical Debate."[30] This article took on national implications, becoming, as one scholar put it, "one of the most widely read and intensely discussed articles of the decade," because it clarified the stakes of debates within Biblical hermeneutics by arguing that resistance to "ruling conventions of exegesis" was "in fact a reaction against what is perceived as the ruling class."[31] Then, in 1987, Lategan coauthored *The Option for Inclusive Democracy,* which contended that a nonracial, inclusive, and pluralistic democracy was more in line with Christian norms than the apartheid system.[32] In the same year, his wife, Esther, ran an unsuccessful campaign as an independent candidate for Stellenbosch in the parliamentary elections. And in 1989, he published a call for social action based on a "new understanding of society" that might emerge from "creative and imaginative theological thinking."[33] When, also in 1989, he signed a sequel to the Kairos Document called "The Road to Damascus," his conservative colleagues at Stellenbosch decided they had had enough, and demanded that he un-sign the document. When he refused, his right to teach in the theological faculty at Stellenbosch was withdrawn.

The increasing social unrest during this time had a particular kind of impact on Biblical scholars, who had provided religious sanction for practices now being judged by the world and by many in their own ranks to be essentially and deliberately unjust. Some of these scholars were now confronting the fact that their work, undertaken perhaps in good but deeply misguided faith, had enabled evil, contributing to the apartheid regime a clean conscience and a sense of righteousness, even sanctity. For them, the enveloping social crisis came to a crunching focus on their own work, and in particular on their use of textual evidence. The gathering consensus in the DRC was that the Bible had been misinterpreted, misused, or misrepresented for reasons that could not be attributed solely to an overzealous faith or honest mistakes. Whether errors in scholarship had been responsible for misreadings that had social and political consequences, or errors in political and moral judgment had distorted their scholarship, was a question few could, or perhaps wished to, answer with certainty. But something had gone terribly awry. The conventions of scholarship, as I suggested earlier, encourage the staging of self-flattering displays of humility in which a scholar confesses that his preconceptions were disproven by the evidence; but in this case, many scholars were coming to the inescapable conclusion that their preconceptions, and consequently their conclusions, were devoutly held, stoutly defended, and actually, horribly wrong.

For Lategan, suspicions about the moral character of the apartheid regime preceded any misgivings about the soundness of his scholarship. During his years (1969–1977) at the University of the Western Cape, surrounded by members of the Dutch Reformed Mission Church, Lategan had been amazed to find that he was treated with an unexpected—even in retrospect an undeserved—decency and respect as a member of the faith community, his conservative views and apartheid background notwithstanding.[34] Over time, such experiences picked away at his deeply held belief that the differences between groups were ineradicable and irreconcilable, and made him responsive to a different view.

His convictions about the divinely ordained diversity of creation were further eroded by his growing understanding of the religious practices of people outside his own group. With riots and violence all around, including a student uprising at his own university in 1973, Lategan observed and read about Bible study groups led primarily by women in the Dutch Reformed Mission Church. These groups, he discovered, were not extracting from the Bible lessons about separate spheres, forced segregation, and the natural dominance of certain groups; instead, they were discovering, in a spirit of profound moral originality, principles and models of perseverance, resistance, healing. They read the Bible as a means of obtaining what Lategan described as a "direct access to the Spirit."[35] As he later wrote, Lategan recognized in these uncredentialed vernacular reading practices a perhaps naïve but compellingly literal understanding of a real, inclusive community of faith, which contrasted sharply with his own comments on the "invisible"—that is, not actually existing and in fact exclusive—community. "A reading in the Spirit," Lategan wrote in 1996, "empowers not only women in a special way, but all people of different religions, cultures, classes, races and gender. . . . The readings of ordinary people in this way form part of a process to restore God's diverse creation and to bring it to fulfillment."[36]

The women in these study groups were not scholars, but then Paul was not writing to a community of university-trained theologians, so in a sense the women could be said to have a more direct access not just to the Spirit but to the text and the intentions behind the text than any professor; and their readings could claim to have greater legitimacy than the tedious, hyper-scrupulous, and, as it now appeared with increasing clarity, essentially vicious pronouncements coming from the Church. The rediscovery of the text, or the discovery of new meanings within the text, was, for Lategan, accompanied by the discovery of the reader, or readers.

Over the course of the critical period of the 1980s, Lategan had become increasingly engaged with Continental hermeneutics, drawing from a wide range of theories that stressed reception and the role of the reader. References to Jacques Derrida, Hans Robert Jauss, the Prague School, pragmatics, reception theory, North American reader response theory, and Wolfgang Iser and the Constance School began to appear in his work. But whereas many North American academics were inferring from the plethora of theoretical movements a general destabilization of meaning—there was nothing outside the text, but the text was an unmappable, unmasterable wilderness of contradictions and cross-purposes—Lategan saw the opposite: he saw the text being read, effectively, confidently, and charitably, to good effect in the world, by readers who should be considered not as mere recipients of the message but as co-creators.

The work of Paul Ricoeur became particularly important in this respect. Ricoeur himself expressed little interest in the internal ideological debates of the apartheid era in South Africa, or in Biblical hermeneutics generally, but his account of the text and the "conflict of interpretations" surrounding it was, Lategan realized, immensely useful and illuminating in the South African context.[37] Lategan understood that Ricoeur's work broke the stranglehold of the concept, legitimated by both religious fundamentalism and then-fashionable theoretical orthodoxy, of the text as a bounded entity, sealed within its own borders. Describing the origin of the static text as a dynamic "event" that could in principle be re-experienced by readers, Ricoeur effectively unbound the text, making it possible to integrate reading and readers—including marginalized, powerless, and "unintended" readers—into a fuller account of the text and its effects. In Ricoeur's work, texts were considered as worldly objects, invitations to creative reading extended to anyone who could make a good-faith effort at understanding. The guarantor of validity in interpretation was not conformity to scholarly consensus but the good faith in which the effort to understand was made. "Understanding," Lategan wrote, quoting Ricoeur, "does not consist of merely repeating the original speech event. It is 'to generate a new event beginning from the text in which the initial event has been objectified.'"[38]

The wall surrounding the text had been breached. Women's readings, feminist interpretations, liberation theologies, and non-Western theologies including the "public theology" of Desmond Tutu and Beyers Naudé were not, in the terms Ricoeur made available, irrelevant fantasies fluttering around an indifferent and nonresponsive text, but worldly activations of real but dormant elements in the text. This expansion of the concept of the text would prove to be the core of Lategan's contribution. Where Naudé, following the Sharpeville Massacre of 1960, had declared that there was no Biblical warrant for apartheid (an assertion of independence for which he was eventually defrocked and "banned," or subject to house arrest from 1977 to 1984), Lategan, a generation later, went a step further by declaring that the Bible—construed now as the text and its various readings—actually supported the overthrow of an exclusive and oppressive social order. The implications of understanding freely creative reading not as a problem to be overcome but a goal to be aspired to extended well beyond the act of reading itself.[39] Not only was the text itself now teeming with possibilities, but people long accustomed to drawing inspiration and authority from the Bible could feel that the values of openness and dynamism were supported by textual evidence.

In responding so enthusiastically to alternative readings achieved by hitherto marginalized readers, Lategan clearly saw himself not as rejecting scholarship but as following a scholarly imperative by reading closely, attending carefully, and submitting the text to the most advanced methods scholarship had developed. The history of scholarship could in fact be read in a way that would support such a claim. Among the earliest triumphs of modern scholarship was the discovery in the eighteenth century of the historicity of the Biblical text. This premise matured over the course of the nineteenth century into the "historical-critical" method, an orientation toward the text that was eventually extended to the historicity of reading and to an understanding of readerly reception as the most expansive unfurling of the text's semiotic potential. In this meta-narrative, the progress of scholarship and theory could be seen as arcing toward a generous and worldly understanding of the untheorizable and unpredictable progress of the text through time and space. With only a little imagination—and Lategan certainly had more than a little—one could see modern scholarship beginning with Biblical hermeneutics and ending, at least to date, with what Greenblatt calls social energy, a factor of volatility that only increases as the text circulates, as Lategan put it, "from one cultural context to another, from its original readers to other and new readers."[40]

These theoretical considerations, grounded in political and moral awakenings, informed Lategan's ongoing study of the Bible, and the text of Paul's Letter to the Galatians in particular. With his earlier apartheid reading, which focused on the freedoms enjoyed by the community of the faithful, now seeming decidedly suspect, he returned to the text in the hope that new needs in the present might open up a new organ for understanding the past, and that the ancient text might yield new insights, arguments, and principles.

Under the pressure of events, Lategan discovered points of identification with the apostle that had lain dormant in his own thinking. The first was that he, like Paul, was engaged in an act of interpretation and public persuasion. One of Lategan's most attentive and sympathetic readers noted that in his 1967 dissertation, Lategan had already planted the seed of the later emphasis on reading and worldly activity when he noted that in Paul's Letter, the earthly Jesus appears only in an "indirect" and "interpreted" form, the form given him in Paul's account.[41] At the very beginning of his career, in other words, Lategan had recognized in the Bible itself the centrality of interpretive reading, a dynamic communication process whose implications it would take him a generation to begin to realize.

Lategan's mature understanding of Paul's Letter did not emerge immediately, inevitably, or organically, but followed on the discovery of a second point of identification with Paul, who was dramatically converted on the road to Damascus. In a 1978 essay, Lategan had noted the centrality to the Letter of conversion, and the power of the Word to break human resistance. A decade later, himself breaking away from his attachments and in a sense from his former identity, Lategan rendered this feature of the text in slightly but crucially different terms, meditating on Paul's statement that "the gospel is not according to a human" (Gal. 1:11): "By 'human' or 'normal standards' Paul's own conversion and his call to apostleship . . . are unthinkable. The unexpected, unusual nature of the gospel does not only concern Paul's apostleship, but the whole Christian community. The Christian experience was consistent with God's ways, it was granted against human expectation, in disregard of human standards, without human merits—by grace alone, as 'new creation.'"[42] The difference between 1978 and 1988 is subtle but profound: the power of God, in the earlier text simply an irresistible force before which the human will must give way, is now directed at a total renovation of the human world, a leap into an unknowable futurity.

The introduction of the reader had volatized the Biblical text in one way, detaching it from the control of the author and the authorized reader, cracking it open and exposing it to creative vernacular understandings. But in the 1988 formulation, the emphasis on conversion applies not just to a text or a reader but to a much broader field. The Bible becomes not a transcendent authority for a static order controlled by a national church, but a commanding argument against all current man-made arrangements. In suggesting that the test of faith was the capacity to imagine and embrace an entirely different reality, Lategan was arguing—with evidence drawn from the Bible, evidence that serious people had to take seriously—that those clinging to the old order had not yet read the Word, they had not submitted themselves to it in a proper spirit of humility, they were not yet truly "reformed."

Ricoeur had spoken in *Interpretation Theory* of how texts, outliving their moment and place of origin and offering themselves to multiple identifications, suggested a world in process, a world capable of metamorphosis and change, a world oriented toward the future, a world of possibility—a world, as Lategan now understood, whose central fact was conversion. Lategan had taken this account in a utopian spirit and mapped it onto the South African situation, urging his readers to meditate on the example of Paul, who had experienced a transformation that had seemed impossible, until it happened. And then, at a certain, once-unimaginable moment, Nelson Mandela was released from prison, the African National Congress was unbanned, and a nonviolent transfer of power was begun. The connection between the gospel and the world became clear and strong. And the uniquely authoritative spirit of religion, once conscripted for repression, could now be enlisted in the cause of freedom.

One of the most remarkable aspects of this extraordinary story is the fixed place in Lategan's thinking of Paul's Letter to the Galatians, which served as supporting evidence for two utterly opposed arguments. Discovering the evidence for the new, anti-apartheid meaning in the Letter undoubtedly cost Lategan a great deal of effort, and forced him to renounce and even denounce his earlier scholarship. It would surely have been much easier simply to reject the analogy between the Israelites and the Afrikaners, to abandon the "archeological" understanding of the state, or even to dismiss the Bible as a source of evidence for anything in the present world. A different kind of scholar might have declared that the study of ancient texts does us little good in the urgent here and now, and that we should govern our lives on the basis of fundamental moral convictions and practical political judgments. A different kind of scholar might have confessed to being weak but not wicked, suggesting that he had secretly harbored doubts about apartheid in his heart all along even while reading the Bible in a way consistent with apartheid and with the consensus of the local scholarly community. But Lategan's direct acknowledgment of his apartheid past, and his insistence on retaining his faith in God and his trust in the Bible as a singularly authoritative source of wisdom and guidance, have enabled him to tell a story of exceptional power, especially to his South African audience.

It is Lategan's own story, and he offers it for the nation's consideration. But it is also the story of scholarship itself. If he were to narrate his intellectual history in very general terms, he might say, "I began my efforts to understand the Word of God many years ago with a set of convictions and assumptions given to me by my family, my community, and my church, but I was compelled by the evidence to reject these and embrace a new and entirely different set. The conclusions presented here are not those I would at first have chosen, but they are ones I must embrace. My change is a change of heart but also a simple acceptance of reality. Paul converted; so must we all."

Reflecting on his lifetime of engagement with Paul's Letter to the Galatians, Lategan has said that he cannot decide with any finality whether his evolving political understanding led him to new recognitions about the text, or whether a greater attention to alternative readings of the text enabled by new developments in hermeneutical theory had given him the courage to change his political views. "My own understanding," he wrote in 1999, "is that the latter was triggered by the former. At the same time, without the discovery of the alternatives in the text, it would probably not have been possible to make the shift in a context where the text still exercises persuasive power."[43] In this carefully ambiguous formulation, he credits the power of the reader to create the evidence by which he is compelled, but also insists that the evidence is there to be discovered. He gives a very slight preference, as a scholar must, to discovery over creation.

In 1999, Lategan founded the Stellenbosch Institute for Advanced Study, a research institute modeled on organizations such as the Institute for Advanced Study at Princeton, the Center for Advanced Study in the Behavioral Sciences at Stanford, the National Humanities Center in North Carolina, the Wissenschaftskolleg zu Berlin, the Swedish Collegium, and others, all of which are dedicated to supporting independent research in a nonhierarchical, open environment. The Stellenbosch Institute was built at Mostersdrift, the site of the first settler farm given out by the Cape Dutch Colony in 1679 and therefore in a sense the geographical starting point of Afrikaner presence in the Cape. The idea behind the Institute, Lategan said, was "to acknowledge history and turn it around" by creating "a kind of neutral territory, a thinking space where we would like to invite other people, other universities, other countries to come and help us think about what is good for the country, what is good for science, what is good for intellectual life." In November 2018, the Stellenbosch Institute for Advanced Study announced the appointment of a new rector, Professor Edward Kirumira of Makerere

University. On assuming office, Professor Kirumira said, "We talk about decolonialities and Africanisation but how do we put them into practice? I see myself as part of that experiment." "It should happen here," Kirumira added, "and will probably make much more impact than elsewhere. I hope it can be seen as part of reconstructing. Scholars have a responsibility to reconstruct."[44]

Today, South Africa is a changed and changing country. Not all of the aspirations that arose in the wake of apartheid have been realized, and many have in fact been cruelly disappointed. Some people have despaired or grown cynical. In such a situation, which is after all a local version of a general recognition that the world does not conform to our wishes or hopes, a valuable and even invaluable resource is the sense of possibility—of openness, unpredictability, and contingency—provided by careful study of the record of the past. Scholarship does not by itself convert persons or generate social change, much less reveal the mind of God; but through its faithful transmission of the evidence, and the precious germ of freedom embedded in the evidence, it can help.

CHAPTER THREE

Virgin Vision

Scholarship and the Birth of the New

A GIFTED GIRL in a culturally sophisticated, intellectually advanced, and politically serious household, with many books; a frequent visitor to theaters, libraries, concert halls. The museums are full of objects that she thinks of as ghosts of the past, all assembled for inspection and rumination. Ferociously bookish, she would love to speak with the dead. At twelve, she begins a poem in which she imagines communing with the figures in the museum, including an Egyptian princess: "We are the past," they say to her, "the dead reincarnate." There are so many more of the dead than the living, and their ranks are growing every day! Things speak to her about their owners or creators, about things she wants to learn about, and even about herself.

A thirteen-year-old has much to learn. The museum is much better than *National Geographic* or her grandfather's *Medical Journal* on the subjects of breasts, penises, buttocks, and sex in general. With regard to the "in general," so are the park, the bus, the movie theater, and the apartment-house roof, all places frequented by what she and her friends call fiends. The museum has fewer fiends, but an abundance of the fiendish: St. Erasmus's bowels torn out by some kind of machine, a hook on a spit; St. Agatha's breasts cut off and served on a silver tray; St. Sebastian, pierced by arrows from all angles and yet mysteriously thoughtful. In a book, she comes upon Jean Fouquet's *Virgin of Melun,* which depicts Mary's uncovered breast and, surrounding her, an entourage of scarlet angels nearly splitting out of their shiny skins like little gods of erection.

She develops advanced but somewhat disturbing tastes. Mathias Grünewald's Isenheim Altar, with its greenish, bruised, tortured body of Christ on the cross was not a common discussion subject in her Jewish household, but it held her imagination in its gothic grip. She also admires Bellini, Picasso, Joyce, Dostoevsky, Tolstoy, O'Neill, Ibsen, Gide, Delmore Schwartz, and Cocteau. She learns French, Latin, and German. She studies piano to play Bach, and paints in the impressionist style.

Passionate on the subject of justice, she is hungry for everything, disgusted by nothing except treacly represen-tations of femaleness: she pokes the eye out of Tinkerbell in an expensive edition of *Peter Pan.* In the realm of art, nothing offends her; nothing seems to her ugly or distorted in itself. She is radically exposed to art and aspires to be a poet, a dancer, a painter. At twelve, she reads *The Magic Mountain* in a day and a night, by sunlight and flashlight, translating Clavdia Chauchat's French herself.

Off to college, one of the Seven Sisters, majoring in philosophy, followed by a master's in seventeenth-century literature. At the age of twenty-three, she is offered a replacement position in art history at her college, and takes it. Somewhat to her surprise, she likes the work, and decides to enter a PhD program. She marries, and has a daughter.

A worldly person, she focuses in her graduate studies on realism in art. But she has interests, abilities, and appetites beyond realism, beyond art history, and beyond academe. She wants to write a novel, perhaps something in the manner of Gide's *The Counterfeiters*. This, she decides, requires a trip. Somewhere. She goes to Colmar in France, checks into a small hotel near the town center, and spends a turbulent week in the colossal presence of Grünewald's altar.

For five days, she drinks in Grünewald's genius. She wants to write, to convert her thoughts and feelings into language, but no genre or category of writing offers itself as adequate. Staring at the central panel showing the Crucifixion, she begins. "It is by the contours that the distinctive quality of each suffering is conveyed," she writes, "with precise and stirring differentiation. For instance, compare the quivering, delicately lumpy contour of the Magdalene's face with the no less sensitive but stronger, more fibrous outline of Christ's body." Her penetrating, decomposing gaze drifts downward to the feet of Christ, "twisted roots of suffering, stringy, pulpy and tobacco-colored like the old useless roots that appear above the ground, patient with toadstools, all sinews and puffs." The little toe of that impaled foot is, she notices, "painted in curving roundels of flesh, like a lamb-chop; the spike is cruel and ignorant as the butcher's hook, and over it the blood slowly pours down."

What is this? Who cares? Something new is being brought into the world, growing under her pen.

The second set of panels in the triptych, so much going on: the Annunciation, the Virgin and Child, a Heavenly Choir, the Resurrection. Her eye comes to rest on the humblest and least meaningful objects in the composition: a tub, a cradle, an angel's viol, all of which, it seems to her, "share in the same palpable quality of material—blanched, grainy, soft-looking wood, wood as though lovingly rubbed and rubbed by cherishing, fore-warming hands, blanched, bleached to the basic bones of woodenness, wood that no longer has anything to do with trees, but only with curving, holding, being held, touched, rubbed." The angel's viol reminds her for some reason "of a churn, Le Nain's churn, I think it is," or maybe "Chardin's leather fountain, some galettes on a plate of Monet, although I am not sure that this is quite the same thing." Have to look that up sometime, she thinks. Meanwhile, galettes: a good word, elegant and gallant baked in a pie.

Writing with constant reference to the painting like an apprentice copying masterpieces in a museum, she pores over the monsters attacking St. Antony: "scaly-plated-prickly in the foreground, like an armadillo; then feathery-beaky; then a roguish simian type in a ragged red cap, snot bubbling from his nose; then a rubbery fungoid alligator, incongruously fitted with wings, like a flying toadstool . . . one with elephant's trunk and streaming human eyes, a corrupted Dumbo." And the image of the Virgin in the aedicula (a word that pleases the mouth), with her yellow hair, "which is really the light into which she has been transmuted."

And finally—because there must be finality: "Every great artist must have his obsession. . . . Grünewald's is a ravening desire for the detailed face of creation: everything is acceptable, adorable, proper to the domain of living art. Nothing in creation, no matter how loathsome or humble, is found lacking or unworthy. . . . His was a total affirmation that confronted and transformed the tumultuous up-rush of things as they are."

Exhausted, exhilarated, replete with sensation but depleted of energy, she returns home, where her daughter and her unfinished dissertation on Courbet's realism greet her. The novel will have to wait.

What a week. In a sense, it was nothing, just an intensified experience of the altar, which she'd studied in books. She had learned nothing, except, perhaps, about experience and intensification themselves. But these had effects that could be considered knowledge about the ways that mere paint can rouse the mind and body, creating a disturbance that can then take linguistic form that translates the paint into thoughts, her own and the painter's, and how this translation gives her ownership of the experience and grants the painter and his work renewed life in another dimension, and how the entire operation can transform the viewer from a passive, gaping admirer into the creator of a new thing. You only really learn about yourself, she reflects, when you leave the shelter of familiar scenes and set out to explore an uncaring world.

This is all very muddy, and nobody but herself could understand it or care. And some dereliction had been involved in the entire adventure. In the end, all she had was the memory of an act of pure selfishness. Her impatient dissertation director and her daughter, each in their own ways, were saying as much. She had traded her worldly responsibilities for precious experience—but she would not have traded that experience for the world.

And these feverish handwritten pages she had carried back with her. Inadmissible in a graduate school context, and utterly useless in any other. She had tied up her experience in a little golden sack that opened to herself alone. There was something powerful and new, and yet—and she realized this now—also something impotent and private about them. She had performed a kind of rapture-experiment, staring and writing without scholarly constraint or rational limitation. It was fine, in its way, but it was strictly personal, psychological, centered—womanly in the worst way, the apolitical way she had always rejected. It went nowhere. It was all about details, fragments. It criticized nothing, changed nothing, gave birth to nothing but itself. Maybe some dinky little press no one ever heard of would publish a few copies. But this would not advance the cause of justice, or even her own cause, which come to think of it might be retarded or even reversed by publication. She wanted something more. She wanted influence, she wanted to make a mark, to pry things open; she wanted to change minds, change the world. She wanted something different, something more direct, something that could get a better purchase on things, something less lubricious. Strong word.

She wanted . . . footnotes.[1]

Footnotes. The most hateful, risible, off-putting, vermiculate feature of scholarship. The fine-print hideaway for caution, boasting, temerity, ass-covering, and intimidation. The ramifying fungal symptom of a disease of scholarship, the death-drive of knowledge, a dark and airless basement for castoffs and junk, the swarming anthill of micro-disputation, the Great Dismal Swamp of irrelevance, the graveyard of readerly interest, eloquent evidence of a wasted life spent in the pointless pursuit of the not-worth-pursuing. A crushed but rebellious force whose mad ambition is plainly to rise up and crowd the "main" (read: entitled) text off the page altogether so that recto and verso are *all note,* a sublime result approached only by a few geniuses (Friedrich Nietzsche, *On the Genealogy of Morals;* F. A. Wolf, *Prolegomena to Homer*) and inspired parodists (David Foster Wallace, *Infinite Jest*).[2] An anti–Mardi Gras inversion where unashamed pedantry overthrows and mocks the vulgarly populist argument. *Who's in charge now, Professor?* All the eyesore forms taken by the scholar's secret desire to leave the world, go underground, burrow in among the worms, insects, and rodents, and stay there without having resolved the question or advanced the issue.

That said, footnotes are the defining mark of modern scholarship. Indeed, they can be considered a pinhole, a tiny aperture through which the entirety of modern scholarship can be viewed—an Ansatzpunkt, as Panofsky put it; a point of departure.

A deep history of the footnote might include forms of commentary and annotation in the ancient world, glosses of holy scriptures, explanatory remarks printed with secular texts—all the forms of citation and annotation that appear in books or manuscripts from time immemorial. But as Anthony Grafton argues in the deep history that he did in fact write, *The Footnote: A Curious History,* none of these slides easily into the distinctive form of the footnote, whose origin he puts at about 1700.[3] The Homer of the genre— that is, the first truly great and in a sense unsurpassable master—was, Grafton claims, Pierre Bayle, whose *Historical and Critical Dictionary,* begun in the 1690s, consists largely of footnotes, and even footnotes to footnotes, offering the reader "only a thin and fragile crust of text on which to cross the deep dark swamp of commentary" (191).

According to Grafton, the citational practice that Bayle thought made his work radically new also made it, in the eyes of some contemporaries, irritating and scandalous, just as Bayle's overall project of exposing the errors in all previous scholarship was condemned as a vast engine of impiety undermining Protestantism, the Bible, and the very possibility of certain knowledge. But, like footnotes themselves, the practice proliferated, and by midcentury footnotes were sufficiently well established as a feature of scholarly practice that they could be satirized. In 1759,

Laurence Sterne published the first volume of *Tristram Shandy*, which included footnotes referring to learned meditations on, for example, the conflicting claims of venerable authorities on the means of christening before birth.[4] One note provides an extensive summary of scholarly debate over the centuries, all sources cited in Latin abbreviations, on whether the phrase "Promontory of Noses" refers to an actual place or is merely an allegorical expression "importing no more than that nature had given him a long nose: in proof of which, with great learning, he cited the underwritten authorities"—who, however, disagree among themselves, leaving the issue, after much erudite disputation, unsettled (179).

But the potential for the ridiculous and even the contemptible that haunts the footnote did not prevent scholars from claiming the mysterious form of authority the footnote could confer. Five years before *Shandy* appeared, David Hume began to publish what would become his six-volume *History of England from the Invasion of Julius Caesar to the Revolution in 1688*. Hume's practice is not nearly as festive or literary as the more celebrated examples from Gibbon—the Shakespeare of the form, whose *History of the Decline and Fall of the Roman Empire* did not begin to appear until 1776—and most of his notes are merely references to sources, but his few attempts at discursive footnotes already capture the essence. Hume says, for example, that when, in 1386, Parliament demanded that Richard II return to London from Eltham, where he had taken refuge from forces hostile to him, the king at first protested, but changed his mind and returned. But Hume does not simply assert this; he provides a footnote to a contemporary source, an account written by a Leicester clergyman named Henry Knyghton that is now known as the fifth volume of *Knighton's Chronicon* or *Chronicle* (c. 1395): "Knyghton, p. 2715, &c."[5] Why does Hume bother to cite Knyghton, and what is implied by the citation?

First, the note suggests that truth is the result of labor, not inheritance or divination. The source for the claim about the king's travels had to be sought out and read in order to become a source, so Hume implicitly represents himself as a person who has done that job, and then done another, more artisanal kind of craftwork in assimilating Knyghton's account into his own narrative of the history of England. The author of a footnote is not a mere writer, much less an oracle or a man of effortless wisdom, but a specific and individual worker—"David Hume, Esq." Brilliantly composed and eminently readable, Hume's *History of England* qualifies as a literary artifact of a very high order, but the footnotes make of it something else in addition—an account with claims on the truth that might be verified by consulting the sources—Knyghton and all his sources, all of whose labor fertilizes Hume's account. Everything about the footnote suggests work of a certain kind, performed by what would eventually be called a professional in the field of scholarly research.

Second, the note suggests an empirical observation of evidence. Hume has not been content merely to repeat what others have said—that the king went from London to Eltham and back again—but has revisited one of the primary sources of such traditional accounts and has personally examined it in order to see what it actually said. He would not have done so if he had not felt that a fresh look at Knyghton's chronicle might yield new discoveries or insights. The source is, in other words, treated as a pristine spring uncontaminated by centuries of repetition and unintentional or perhaps intentional deformation. The near-contemporaneity of Knyghton's account with the king's trip increases the likelihood that the king really did travel from Eltham to London at the request of Parliament, and diminishes the possibility that the account of that trip was deformed or contaminated by some political or moral agenda. The *Chronicon* comes close to being the kind of "genuine and original document" that Ranke prized as the best source of information for the scholar, and its incorporation into the text anchors Hume's account in observed fact. Even if Knyghton himself had not seen the king and his retinue passing on the road, he might have known some who had; but the more important fact is that Hume had personally examined Knyghton's book.

The direct observation of evidence creates the distinctive sense of veracity that defines modern scholarship. What Grafton calls a "traditional" (i.e., footnote-less) work of scholarship might be commended or condemned on the basis of its style, its general sense of command, its conformity with received opinion and with the interests of those currently in power. As Grafton says, "Traditional political historians, in the ancient world and in the Renaissance, wrote from within a rhetorical tradition, as statesmen or generals address their peers. The histories they produced reflected far more interest in virtue and vice than in sources and dating" (23). But a work of modern scholarship asks to be judged on its fidelity to the truth, however that term is construed, and this fidelity can be judged most directly by examining the sources used by the scholar to see if they are accurately represented. The real focus in a work of modern scholarship is not on the charm of the style or the agreeability of the argument but on the handling of the sources, and it is in the footnotes that the reader finds the materials he would need to judge how well the scholar has done his job.

This kind of citizen's verification was important to Hume because his goal was not just to please, delight, or edify, but to persuade. His history was not a mere chronicle of events but an argument that he wished to command attention and expected to be controversial: that the English Constitution, not the monarchy, was the site of ultimate authority. Hume wanted to embed this argument into English national self-understanding so that future decisions would be made on this basis. If he were to have the kind of influence he desired, he would have to overcome resistance from those who took a different view of the rebellion of 1688, the monarchy, or the Tory party. Hume certainly knew that many opponents of his argument would attack him personally, and footnotes provided some defense by enabling him to refer critics to his sources as the basis for his argument.

Footnotes constitute, then, a proleptic defense against criticism. But at a deeper level, they mark the aspiration to originality. Their implicit, iconoclastic message is,

"Previous writers have gotten things wrong, and *here is the proof.* As any fair-minded person can see, the sources on which any account must be constructed were misinterpreted or ignored altogether. A fresh, honest reading reveals the dimensions of their irresponsibility and provides the basis for the true account herein presented." This scholarly ambition to differ, to improve, and to innovate has roots in two of the most fertile fields of modernity. Grafton suggests that in a Protestant culture virtue naturally "associates itself with claims of novelty and reform," but the act of turning to the source in a spirit of direct empirical observation owes as much to science, with its orientation toward discovery and originality, as to religion (229). Odd and even bizarre though it sounds, footnotes represent a general spirit of modernity that actually appropriates elements of both religion and science.

Religion and science represent forms of authority, but the concept of sources suggests a principle of mediation. The past does not speak for itself; the dead do not converse with us. All we can know directly are after-effects or traces, and even these have their mysteries and secrets. Knyghton is one such trace, but no number of Knyghtons will saturate the field so that one can speak with complete assurance that one possesses the whole truth and nothing but the truth. Indeed, modern scholarship has uncovered no less than 110 (largely unacknowledged) sources that Knyghton himself drew on.[6] The scholar must harvest his argument from his sources, but every source contains potentially resistant elements that could be conscripted in the service of a different argument. Guesswork and speculative infills are the essence of the scholar's work, no matter how many or how rich the sources may be, and in fact increase with the number and quality of sources.

The point in the present context is that the use of sources provides the scholar with both observable facts and a mandate to massage, supplement, or otherwise interpret these facts. In a work of modern scholarship, the source is treated not as an unimpeachable authority, but as a contribution to an account that includes and exceeds it. The scholar is always in the ambivalent position of both presenting and diverging from the evidence. Hume understands the necessity of what would come to be called a "critical" perspective on his sources, and so after citing Knyghton, he continues: "The same author, p. 2680, tells us, that the King, in return to the message, said, that he would not for their desire remove the meanest scullion from his kitchen. . . . But it is plain, that all these speeches were either intended by Knyghton merely as an ornament to his history, or are false" (251). Even as he claims the authority of Knyghton for his own account, then, Hume criticizes him as a partisan, sympathetic to Edward III but decidedly less so to Richard II, whose obduracy in the face of Parliament's insistence Knyghton has deliberately overstated.

All this claiming and criticizing are directed toward the reader, who assumes a far different and more active role in the reception of a footnoted text than in the traditional text. So repellant to the eye, the footnote actually represents a gesture toward conversation with a reader whose understanding and assent are being courted. Notes signify that the reader is considered a qualified judge, a person who, given time and resources, might do a fact check or even challenge the scholar's account; indeed, citing the sources for one's argument almost dares the reader to disprove it. Collegiality, courtesy, a presumption of equality—a general democracy of knowledge—are all implied by the scholar's gesture of sharing his sources and even his reflections on those sources with a public whose legitimate resistance to an original argument is assumed and respected.

The footnote identifies the context of scholarship as a social world of assertions and exchanges, with a presumption of a common competence. The traditional text addresses the reader from the stage, treating the reader as the audience to a performance, capable of judging the work's effect on him- or herself but not its veracity or its adequacy to its subject. The footnoted text, by contrast, addresses the reader in his freedom as a coequal, a person who submits willingly if skeptically to a process of argumentation.

The footnote introduces, then, several factors of difference into scholarly discourse—between the source and the scholarly inference, the source and the ultimate truth, and the author and the reader. Most conspicuously, the footnote divides the scholarly text into the main argument, which slides along gracefully on top, and the bottom-dwelling notes, which record the scholar's research "like an engineer's diagram of a splendid building," as Grafton puts it (23). The footnotes make the otherwise obscure process by which the scholar arrived at his conclusions almost visible, enabling the reader to speculate about the alchemy that transmuted doubtful or fragmentary sources into arguments with a purchase on the truth. This kind of readerly speculation can be strangely rewarding and even stimulating. Grafton concludes his history with warm words of appreciation for "the most elaborate set of historical footnotes ever written—a set of four layers, footnotes to footnotes to footnotes to footnotes" in a 1934 publication of the Warburg Institute that "provided a written counterpart to the experience of working in the Warburg library itself, where the encounter with traditions juxtaposed in radically new ways was meant to shock readers into creativity."[7]

But perhaps the most interesting and most decisive difference effected by the footnote is in the authorial voice itself. A scholarly argument represents itself as the definitive treatment of its subject—the best, most responsible, most well defended argument possible at the present time. It tends and intends to daunt. But the discursive footnote, speaking in a second voice typically pitched in a different register from the main text, introduces a potentially ludic or even comic difference into the authorial persona, separating the scholar from himself. In many cases, the voice of the note is less formal than that of the main text, with the author appearing out of costume, as it were, to address the reader in a more direct and familiar tone, perhaps with the humanizing touch of humor. In others, the voice of the note is (even) drier and less personal than that of the main text. But in all cases, there is a difference. One cannot avoid thinking that one of the voices is the genuine, natural voice of the scholar, while the other is performed, even though it may be impossible to know which is which. A footnoted text is like a ventriloquist with a dummy so realistic that it's not clear which is which.

The text aerated or ironized by discursive footnotes surrenders the kind of authority claimed by science or mathematics or even philosophy, but scholarship based on sources does not proceed by applying rules or following chains of deductions. What it does do is demonstrate in its very form a respect for a conversation based on fact and predicated on difference, an understanding of the multiplicity of truth and even of the self, and an implicit but uncompromised endorsement of the proposition that no final, univocal solution will ever bring the process of inquiry and interpretation to an end. These are among the central premises of scholarship.

As it happens, there was a scholar who bore some resemblance to the woman represented in the imagined scenario with which this chapter began. When Linda Nochlin died in 2017 at the age of eighty-six, she was hailed as a scholar of extraordinary distinction and influence, the author of many influential books and articles, the curator of several landmark exhibitions, and a leading authority on both nineteenth-century realism and contemporary art.[8] Her work was celebrated for its remarkable richness and range, and for its sentence-by-sentence spirit of responsiveness, clarity, and force; it was, as one scholar put it (to her), "unceasingly bold, intrepid . . . transgressive, irreverent, and anti-establishment."[9] Her reputation had, however, for many years been based largely on the fact that she almost singlehandedly founded the field of feminist art criticism, changing the way art was studied, and paving the way for many younger scholars.[10] Because her decisive intervention came at a moment—1971—when "second-wave feminism" was transforming not only other academic disciplines but society at large, Nochlin's work was widely noticed, cited, and circulated. Grounded in fact and framed in nonspecialist terms, the revolution she launched has not dated, and has in fact become as canonical as the works whose status she had called into question. More than most scholars or indeed most people, Linda Nochlin created something new; she changed the world through her scholarship.

But let's return to the beginning. When Nochlin returned from a Fulbright year in France in 1959, she faced the immediate challenge of making a place for herself in the world, a challenge compounded by the death the following year of her husband, the Vassar philosophy professor Philip Nochlin. A single mother, she had a part-time teaching position at Vassar (where she had matriculated in 1951). She was working on a novel (completed but never published), and was commuting to the Institute of Fine Arts at New York University, where she was pursuing her PhD In 1963, she published her impressions of the Isenheim Altar, originally intended as a section of that novel, under the title *Mathis at Colmar* (with Red Dust, a dinky little press no one had ever heard of). The same year, she completed her dissertation on Gustave Courbet, which, like most dissertations, asserts at every moment an earnest

FIGURE 3. Linda Nochlin, c. 1968, *photo George Lange.*

familiarity with scholarly conventions, opening with sentences such as "It is the contention of this dissertation . . ." and "We will try to demonstrate that . . ."[11] Most of the first page is taken up by footnotes. In 1968 she married Richard Pommer, an architectural historian at Vassar; their daughter was born the following year. By 1971, she had written an important book on realism (composed almost entirely during her pregnancy; nominated for a National Book Award), edited two volumes of readings on nineteenth-century art, curated an exhibit on realism at Vassar, and published major pieces on Courbet, Pissarro, Philip Pearlstein, the avant-garde in France, and the history of the museum. She was on fire.

One might expect such an exuberant and idiosyncratic intelligence to become an artist rather than a scholar; or, if a scholar, a student of experimental or avant-garde artists who saw themselves as agitators and revolutionaries. She became a scholar of realism, and it is tempting to think that Nochlin, like many other gifted people before and since, came to a sober understanding of how the world works and renounced her creative aspirations in poetry and painting in favor of worthy, satisfying, but more conventional work, building a resumé in the usual fashion. *Mathis at Colmar* had been, as she later said, "more akin to poetry than scholarship," executed "without scholarly restraint or rational limitation," and so was almost useless in this respect—even, perhaps, a negative credential. Her choice of Courbet's realism as a dissertation topic might seem by comparison a resigned and deflated concession to pragmatic necessity (*Women Artists* [hereafter *WA*], 411; *Mathis at Colmar*, 13).

But Nochlin, who later described *Mathis at Colmar* as "one of my favorite creations," did not see her career in these terms (*WA*, 411). She moved with apparent ease and enthusiasm from ekphrasis—which she defined as the "attempt to make a text capture, reduplicate or bring to life a visual image"—to the disintoxicated professional discourse of scholarship (396). The disciplines of art history and art criticism undoubtedly made this transition easier, since any description of the objects of the field must involve ekphrasis, and some distinguished examples of scholarship were, Nochlin notes, "ekphrastic to the highest degree" (399). In art history, the line between ekphrasis and scholarship is blurred or nonexistent, and the continuities between them enable us to grasp not just the logic of Nochlin's career but also the creative and productive dimension of scholarship as such.

We can begin to establish those continuities by noting that the ekphrastic text is a representation that is accountable to an original. The canonical instance of ekphrasis, Homer's description of Achilles' shield, could not, under the circumstances of the time, be directly compared with the shield itself, but the core of ekphrasis is accurate representation, the rendering of image into language. So, too, in scholarship, the stated goal of establishing, in Ranke's phrase, "wie es eigentlich gewesen," or "how it actually was," indicates the centrality to scholarship of concepts of adequacy, accuracy, and fidelity. Even sophisticated theoretical arguments about the inescapability of a perspectival or nonobjective understanding tacitly exempt themselves from the full implications of this claim. The argument is always grounded in some discovery about perception, cognition, or language; nobody who represents himself as a scholar argues that his gut tells him that all knowledge is irreducibly subjective. Scholarly strictures against the confusion of one's personal views, interpretations, or judgments with the object under consideration suggest that scholarship understands itself to be ekphrastic if not to the highest at least to some degree.

Ekphrasis proceeds by noting details, the small, anomalous, incompletely assimilated elements that, like cathedral gargoyles, retain a certain alienated integrity, demanding to be noticed and described in themselves. Taken as a whole, the Isenheim Altar represents a colossal theological statement of some kind—of what kind, scholars disagree[12]—but Nochlin, in the ekphrastic mode, notices the tub, the cradle, and the gored, mangled feet of Christ—the footnotes, as it were, to the sublime drama of the Passion.

Underscoring the limits of conceptualization, idealization, and even coherence, the work of ekphrasis is primarily critical, calling into question all generalizing, detail-effacing generalizations or concepts. But the ultimate justification of ekphrasis, as of scholarship generally, is not just the demolition of some totalizing concept, but the emergence of some new understanding that can be shown to be heralded or implicit, but not fully comprehended or articulated in the object of study itself. Even at its most granular, ekphrasis not only engenders a fresh apprehension of particulars but suggests new or different concepts or patterns. Ekphrasis begins, then, in a spirit of fidelity but, proceeding through translation and transformation, ends in the creation of something different, something new.

In *Mathis at Colmar,* this new understanding emerges at the very end. Grünewald's ultimate message, Nochlin declares, has nothing to do with theology or metaphysics; it does not concern salvation or redemption; heaven is not the goal. No—in actual fact, Grünewald's underlying project was "a total affirmation that confronted and transformed the tumultuous uprush of things as they are" (35). In this formulation, Nochlin has not only identified Grünewald's ambition but, surely unbeknownst to herself at that time, has also set the terms of her own future scholarly career, which would be marked by a comprehensive spirit of acceptance and responsiveness. She also, I would suggest, outlines the essential mission of scholarship as such: the dual task of confronting and transforming the past, bringing present understanding into greater conformity to the truth and opening up hitherto unknown or unimagined paths to the future. The ravening desire that drives Grünewald drives all scholarship, which seeks to correct or supplement previous understandings by producing new insights based on fresh research or a rethinking of the past, a new understanding of things as they really are.

In short, Nochlin's transition from ekphrasis to scholarship, from creation to commentary, was not as jagged or abrupt, and certainly not as tragic, as it might seem. The transition was further eased, and its essential direction confirmed, by the subject Nochlin chose for her dissertation, Courbet's realism. In the account given in her dissertation, the realist style Courbet practiced from 1848 to 1855 was essentially a form of painterly ekphrasis applied to the material world. Courbet, she writes, rejected standards of the past and replaced them with "standards of honesty, directness, and sincerity," reproducing the face of the world as if it were being seen for the first time, without idealization, heroization, symbolism, prettification, ennoblement, abstraction, or imaginative invention (*Gustave Courbet*, 225). She clearly saw her own work on Courbet as proceeding in the same spirit, and indeed almost said as much in a 2002 essay, when she noted that she had tried throughout her career to "look at the old masters with new eyes, [and] see the great works of the past with virgin vision, as though for the first time" (*WA*, 253). What virginity lacks in sophistication it hopes to make up for in freshness, and Nochlin, who, like other graduate students, perhaps feared that the apprentice work in her dissertation would be found banal, awkward, or inept, may have been trying to stand beside, or behind, the figure of Courbet, whose manifest lack of conventional craft could—as she was arguing—be understood as a principled refusal to repeat the mannerisms of his predecessors in the practice, as she was refusing to repeat the calcified fantasies of previous scholarship.

The key was the details. Nochlin's Courbet, like Nochlin's Grünewald and indeed like Nochlin herself, was obsessed with "the detailed face of creation." The radical but undervalued innovation of realism lay in a startling attention to detail that signified the painter's emancipation from general ideas and guild conventions. What might appear as a process of apparently artless or "additive" composition was in fact a cunning attempt to simulate the hitherto unseen microbia of everyday reality. By including seemingly negligible elements that bore no stamp of meaning, and which had found their way into the composition for no other reason than that reality is made of such stuff, the realist painter displayed an honorable humility in the presence of the real, sacrificing a painterly unity of composition to a higher principle of fidelity to the truth.

Realism may have been ekphrastic in its attention to detail, but for Nochlin realism had something ekphrasis did not, a critical orientation directed not at its subjects but toward the traditional practice of painting. Well into the twentieth century, the nonsignifying dreck of life was considered beneath the notice of the great artist. In 1927, Roger Fry said, "This everyday vision has not been the concern of the greatest painters; they have sought to place themselves at a greater distance from the phenomena of nature. . . . They have sought . . . to discover those more universal truths which escape the untrained vision." Clive Bell added an even more stinging note of condemnation: "Detail is the heart of realism and the fatty degeneration of art."[13] Nochlin disagreed. For her, it was the studied and harmonious compositions of many of the most celebrated artists that were degenerate, while the details of realism signified vigor, vitality, and presence—insubordination in general. "It is," she said in a 1988 essay, "Women, Art, and Power," "only by breaking the circuits, splitting apart those processes of harmonizing coherence . . . that change can take place."[14] By casting off traditional canons of representation, realism as Courbet practiced it cleared the way for the more manifestly antitraditional innovations of Cézanne, Manet, Monet, and Renoir.

As Nochlin's career unfolded, it became apparent that she herself was deeply in sympathy not only with realism's loving attention to detail, but with the revolutionary spirit of the movement. "I loved realist styles from the gut," she said in an interview near the end of her life, "because they refused the rhetoric of grandeur, the perfection and unity of the High Renaissance, in favor of a different kind of magic, that of the detail, the additive, the allure of the specific" (*WA*, 13). In addition to an oppositional attitude and a juicy preference for specifics over generalizations, realism had something else that a young scholar could admire: a certain coldness of approach that could almost be called scientific. Realism, Nochlin argued, was directly linked to the anti-Romantic embrace of science that swept through intellectual and cultural life at the time, conscripting for its cause even painters, some of whom aspired to the scientific virtues of "impartiality, impassivity, scrupulous objectivity, rejection of a priori metaphysical or epistemological prejudice."[15]

The foundational argument of Nochlin's dissertation is, however, that Courbet's realism drew its principles not from science but from the revolutionary turbulence of 1848, and that the formal characteristics of Courbet's painting, which have often been attributed to a primitive or naïve effort simply to imitate nature, in fact and quite deliberately bore social and moral meaning. She contrasted Courbet's documentary attention to appearances not only to the dominant academic milieu but also to the practice of Manet by saying that Courbet is engaged in a "*dialogue* between the means of art and the subject represented," while Manet "conceives of his art as a *monologue* which his subjects interrupt" (*Gustave Courbet,* 229).[16] Courbet's practice is, in other words, social and egalitarian, while Monet's work evokes the undisturbed inner voice of the sovereign

subject. The details for which realism was so sharply criticized by the guardians of taste and craft at the time
stood in for *le peuple*, the marginalized or socially dispos-
sessed figures who were thought to have no place in an artistic composition. And the apparent lack of design in a
composition like Courbet's monumental *Burial at Ornans*,
which depicts its forty-five life-sized figures as a series of
individual portraits rather than as elements in a carefully
assembled arrangement or a coordinated whole, constitutes a "pictorial 'democracy,'" a "compositional *égalitarisme*" (133–34).[17]

For Nochlin's Courbet, realism—the "stalwart confrontation of actuality"—was an argument in paint for democracy, modernity, and the principle of a renovation of
vision based on the truth; for Nochlin herself, scholarship
on Courbet represented a seconding of the motion in the
contemporary world, a rational argument sympathetically
affirming and implicitly endorsing Courbet's political as
well as artistic agenda (*Courbet*, 111). As Courbet had created a new reality in his work, Nochlin aspired to create a
new Courbet.[18]

The agenda Nochlin identified in Courbet was radical
and emancipatory: he had liberated painting from the academies and the salons; he had freed painting from its
bondage to literature and narrative; he had made painting
accountable to the real world rather than to the ingrained
conventions of the guild; he had represented a world
without false grandeur or pretension; he had given ordinary people the kind of dignity and respect hitherto accorded only to figures of privilege or power; and he had

even exposed himself by refusing to represent himself as an accomplished or sophisticated artist, a genius in the mold of Delacroix or David. All these refusals, rejections, and abandonments bore witness to a single, penetrating insight: any lordly claim of an overmastering authority, whether political, social, or artistic, is founded on a wicked illusion that the world would be better off without.

It was as if Courbet, or Nochlin's Courbet, had discovered in the traditional practice of painting a question that had covertly determined its schema of representation, the hidden basis for its conventions. That question was, "Why are ordinary people so uninteresting, unaccomplished, ugly, dull, and disorganized?" The answer was, "They are incapable of being interesting, important, coherent, impressive, or beautiful"—to which the response of the academies was, "Ordinary life can be redeemed only by Genius, which sifts, distills, purifies, and ennobles—and that's where we come in." According to Nochlin's Courbet, the original question was insidious and the answer secreted in it therefore wrong. Both should be abandoned, and another question put in its place: "What kinds of dignity, interest, and value does ordinary life possess, and how can these qualities be rendered in paint?" Realism was the response to this hitherto unasked question.

Although she did not elaborate this point fully at this early moment in her career, it cannot have escaped Nochlin's attention that among the revolutions effected by realism was an altogether new way of depicting women. A woman in a realist painting was not just the Virgin Mary, the wife of a wealthy or powerful man, or a body to be ogled, but, typically, an individual going about the mundane business of life, participating in the daily routines in which traditional painting had taken little interest. Largely confined to these routines in their ordinary lives, women, when they painted, typically worked in the realist mode, creating works that underscored, often ironically, their allotted roles.[19] The realist depiction of women, especially those *by* women, was not, then, simply a passive register of the status quo but a protest against a tradition of painting that had been complicit with the patriarchal traditions and assumptions that regulated the social order.

In retracing the steps in Nochlin's early career, I have been trying to identify the ligatures that could connect a creative practice of ekphrasis that confronted and transformed the image to a scholarly practice that confronted and transformed its objects. The connective link in Nochlin's case is provided by realism, a painterly practice of confronting and transforming the practice of painting and, by implication, the social world surrounding and supporting that practice. In a 2007 essay introducing a collection of her essays on Courbet, Nochlin noted that Courbet's admirers are often "seduced into reading their own obsession or at the very least intense feelings into Courbet's mysterious imagery."[20] This is precisely what I am arguing about Nochlin's own early encounter with Courbet in her dissertation. Establishing through research and analysis the connections between Courbet's style and the ideas of 1848, Nochlin proceeded in the spirit of critical realism she was analyzing, bringing to light a revolutionary political program that actually determined what might have seemed a mere obedient recording of material fact.[21] Describing Courbet as a scholar in paint, she cast herself as a realist in the mode of scholarship.[22]

At the point we have reached—the late 1960s, when she was in her late thirties—Nochlin appeared to consider herself a student of the past. She had identified in the two subjects I have focused on, Grünewald and Courbet, an embrace of the real, of "things as they are." She had noted in these subjects a dual movement of criticism, rejection, and defiance on the one hand, and the generation of the new on the other. She had recognized the critical and germinative role in their work played by hitherto unnoticed or marginalized details. She had identified the principle of the new order signaled by the work of Courbet from 1848 to 1855 as a revolutionary democracy based on the principle of equality. She had allied herself sympathetically with that principle. But she had not yet discovered, much less declared, an argument of her own that would enable her to undertake her own realist revolution in the contemporary world.

That changed abruptly in 1969.

That was the year that, as Nochlin recalled in a 1994 essay called "Starting from Scratch," "I had a baby, I became a feminist, and I organized the first class in Women and Art at Vassar College."[23] The second and third items on that list were precipitated by a question that provoked a mental revolution "rather like the conversion of Paul on the road to Damascus," when a colleague at Vassar gave her a briefcase full of polemical literature and said, "Have you heard about Women's Liberation?" (188).

She hadn't, or at least hadn't heard about "second-wave" feminism; but she plundered that briefcase late into the night, poring over the materials in a state of mounting exhilaration. Her reading crystallized a diffuse sense of rage at her own marginalization—as a Jew, as a woman, as a marginal hanger-on in a marginal department at a small college. She recalled the Tinkerbell incident from her youth, and saw with new clarity what that had meant. She raided Simone de Beauvoir for inspiration. She reflected on the fact that not only the faculty in the art department but all the artists studied in that department—all the artists considered great—were male, while women entered the scene only as models for painters or students for professors. The message of the whole arrangement was that to be an art historian was to immerse oneself to the point of drowning in male achievement, male desire, and male self-celebration. Nobody escaped. Even she herself, toiling away on Courbet and realism. . . . Wasn't reality itself oppressive enough that she had to spend her life staring at pictures of it?[24]

Then, the following year, another question provoked the cascade of revelations that would launch her career and upend the field. At the 1970 Vassar graduation, where Gloria Steinem was the speaker, Nochlin was approached by a gallery owner who said he would love to show women artists, but there weren't any good ones, and why was that?

She thought about it, and over the course of the next few months wrote one of the most influential academic essays in recent times, "Why Have There Been No Great Women Artists?"[25] Every word of this article carries the force of enraged conviction, expressed with a freestyling panache and flung out as if into a high wind of opposition. The argument is commonly praised for its originality, but the basic analytical style was similar to that of her previous work. The very question, she begins, while innocent enough, carries the unspoken assumption that women are incapable of greatness, and merely asks for reasons why this is so. This assumption encrypts a nested series of conceptual errors and social deformities that have corrupted our understanding and our social arrangements for so long that they seem part of the natural order. To take the question seriously, to search for "forgotten flower-painters or David-followers," is, she argued, implicitly to endorse these errors. The search had to be given up: "The fact, dear sisters, is that there are no women equivalents for Michelangelo or Rembrandt . . . any more than there are Black equivalents for the same," or "Lithuanian jazz pianists [or] Eskimo tennis players" (*WA*, 46, 45). Nor should we be looking to discover a different, quieter, more modest or retiring, specifically feminine kind of greatness. The question itself had to be rejected.

One of the most fundamental errors camouflaged by the question about the absence of great women artists is a Romantic conception of art as "the direct, personal expression of individual emotional experience" when in fact, as Nochlin says, art is "a self-consistent language of form [based on] schemata or systems of notation, which have to be learned or worked out, either through teaching, apprenticeship or a long period of individual experimentation" (*WA*, 45). The myth of the great artist is the flower of a deeper and equally mythical myth of artistic genius as a mysterious essence that will find a way to express itself no matter how unpromising the circumstances. Art history, or mythology, is full of anecdotes in which some inconsequential or socially invisible person unexpectedly displays an astonishing untutored gift, as when a lowly shepherd boy draws a perfect circle and, given opportunity, becomes Giotto. The ostensibly factual biographies of many other artists repeat this myth of a natural talent that suddenly and miraculously declares itself during the artist's childhood, provoking everyone to declare the young Picasso, for example, to be a transcendent genius. The absence of such stories, either mythic or modern, about girls seems to prove that they just don't have the gift.

Nochlin's response to this implication was to pose another question: "What if Picasso had been born a girl?" (*WA*, 49). Would her father have paid as much attention to her? Would he have stimulated as much ambition in a daughter as in a son? Would Pablita have been encouraged to apply to the Barcelona Academy of Art? And if by chance she had been admitted, would she have been treated as a miracle and given access to classes, nude models (which, Nochlin points out, were "essential to the training of every young artist [and] to the production of any work with pretentions to grandeur"), apprenticeships, patrons, salons, galleries, intellectual life in general (52)? The question does not wait for an answer, and leads directly to Nochlin's assertion that what we call genius is not a miraculous

natural faculty but "an activity of a subject *in a situation*"—
a situation in which women never find themselves because
they are excluded by deep-laid social conventions from
all activities involving mastery, command, achievement, or a public audience (52). In such a fix, Nochlin concludes, even the most gifted woman artist requires not
just talent but "a good strong streak of rebellion," and the
ability to adopt, "however covertly, the 'masculine' attri-
butes of single-mindedness, concentration, tenaciousness
and absorption in ideas and craftsmanship for their own
sake" (63).

It is a brilliant and inspiring argument that, while revolutionary in some ways, would come to be seen as a
powerful representative of the ethos of the 1970s, in which
the field of art history would be challenged and invigorated
by the concept of social history. But what concerns us in
the present context is not the argument itself, but the privileged place of scholarship in it. The last point, about the
necessity of adopting "masculine" modes for the over-
turning of patriarchal attitudes and institutions, applies
directly here, for while Nochlin condemns male-dominated
scholarship for perpetrating all the misconceptions she
lists, she never condemns scholarship itself, and even advances scholarship as the most effective weapon against
"false consciousness" (*WA*, 68). In a 1974 essay, she was particularly insistent on this point, arguing that the most effective way to topple the patriarchy is "through thought,
through the pursuit of truth, and through the constant
questioning and piercing through of our so-called 'natural'
assumptions."[26]

In fact, Nochlin seems to regard scholarship as a more effective emancipatory force for women than feminism. A fact not often noted in the many references to this path-breaking feminist essay is that it actually begins with complaints about feminism, which, while "liberating," had been "chiefly emotional" in its effects, too focused "on the present and its immediate needs rather than on historical analysis of the basic intellectual issues" (*WA*, 42). Feminism, she almost says, has been too effeminate to effect real change, either of understanding or of social practice. Only scholarship is capable of correcting the intellectual distortions on which traditional social arrangements are founded; only scholarship can bring new facts to light, or, more radically, pose a new set of questions. What is needed is not greater fervor but a "dispassionate, impersonal, sociological, and institutionally oriented approach," a coolly demolishing gaze that lays bare the "conceptual smugness" and "meta-historical naïveté" of the prevailing doctrines, even of feminism, and generally clears the path (42).

Recall that in 1899, Du Bois decided, in the wake of a lynching, that violence rather than ignorance was the problem, and that "the cure wasn't simply telling people the truth, it was inducing them to act on the truth."[27] Nochlin seems to have found this an unnecessary opposition, and took scholarship as a form of social action. Women, she argued, have an advantage in scholarship that they do not have in society. The powerlessness that makes it difficult for women to mount an effective resistance to their own exclusion makes it easier for them to see social or ideological conventions from the outside. When male scholars adopt the persona of the neutral "one," they often delude even themselves into thinking they have surrendered their authority and privilege when they have actually enhanced their already-strong position by merging their perspective with that of humanity in general. Women can assume the outsider's perspective without artifice or deception, and without kidding anyone. Their position as "underdogs in the realm of grandeur, and outsiders in that of ideology" gives women a decided advantage in unraveling the entire skein of prejudicial assumptions about women, art, genius, and nature that sustain the patriarchal order (*WA*, 67).

How can Nochlin argue for a feminist perspective without abandoning the concepts of reality and truth that she very clearly wants to retain? The key to her understanding of this paradox is her account of realist painting as a practice of accurate representation that proceeds from definite social and political commitments held by a particular individual. Reality and truth, she seems to argue, are what appear to someone—some subject in a situation—as convincingly real and true. Women and men read and write from different situations, but all are situated somehow. The primary difference is that to read as a man—that is, unconsciously and in a sense innocently, as if one were not "situated" at all—is to be deceived; to read as a woman, on the other hand, is to embrace situatedness as such, and to do so through a free, deliberate, and provocative choice.

The mighty machine capable of clearing the ground of sedimented misconceptions, the great lever with which scholarship pries thought loose from under the rock of the present, is the question. One of the most conventional things that can be said about scholarship is that (as E. H. Carr does in fact say) "the historian, like any other scientist, is an animal who incessantly asks the question 'Why?'"[28] Carr speaks of putting things in new contexts, interpreting things in new ways, or identifying new things to study, as if the question, itself impenetrable, exposed a certain otherwise unsuspected fragility in all things, but Nochlin's example suggests a deeper level of interrogation in which questions themselves can be exposed to questioning.

In serious and ambitious scholarship, a question may be treated as if it were an answer that may itself be questioned. To the question "Why have there been no great women artists?" the scholar might reply, "Why are you asking that question? Doesn't your question reflect a passive and uncritical acceptance of patriarchal assumptions? Do you actively wish to perpetuate those assumptions and the practices they underwrite or are you simply unaware of what you're doing?" The act of questioning in this case represents an assertion of agency in the face of what seems like necessity, a refusal of assent to propositions others take for granted, a liberating insistence on the possibility of difference even after the doors of possibility have been declared closed.

Questioning is the fundamental gesture of critique, which has always been at the heart of Nochlin's project. "I do not," she has written, "conceive of a feminist art history as a 'positive' approach to the field, a way of simply adding a token list of women painters and sculptors to the canon," but rather, in reading "against the grain, to question the whole art-historical apparatus which contrived to 'put them in their place.'"[29] But she also recognized that this negative, critical work was only a preliminary to a more creative and productive activity in which understanding could be reoriented around a revised and improved understanding of reality. A potentially infinite regress of questioning opens up the possibility of a potentially infinite progress in the pursuit of truth.

The most dramatic instance in Nochlin's oeuvre of this understanding of the creative dimension of scholarship is a two-part 1988 essay called "Courbet's Real Allegory: Rereading *The Painter's Studio,*" a remarkable and, given her empirical commitments, surprising culmination of her decades-long meditation on Courbet.[30] This immense and enigmatic painting, whose full title is *The Painter's Studio: A Real Allegory Summing Up Seven Years of My Artistic and Moral Life,* was executed by Courbet at the end of what Nochlin identified as his realist period, in 1855. It depicts the seated figure of Courbet himself working on a landscape painting, at the center of an assemblage of figures, some identifiable (Baudelaire, Proudhon, Champfleury), others seemingly representative of types, all of them in odd or haphazard postures, and none of them seeming to be interested in or even aware of the others.

Courbet never satisfactorily explained the hidden allegorical meaning of his painting. But modern scholarship has convinced itself that many of the once-anonymous figures clustered on the left side of the painting can be identified and the secret meaning unveiled.[31] That meaning, according to Klaus Herding, is a lesson of peace, harmony, and reconciliation, addressed to Emperor Napoleon III.[32] This dual triumph of research in identifying the figures and determining the meaning of the totality leaves Nochlin dazzled but finally irritated, for, with everything so neatly settled, Nochlin says, "there is nothing left to discover. We have come to the end of interpretation" ("Courbet's Real Allegory," 158). Acknowledging the force of the evidence behind Herding's interpretation, Nochlin yet feels "a surge of rebellion" at the fact that she and other viewers "have been shut out of the house of meaning. The only way I can get back in," she writes, "is by bowing down to authority, and I don't bow easily; in fact, I don't usually bow at all" (158).

It is not just the end of interpretation in this one case that provokes Nochlin, but the concept of allegory itself, which, as the literary scholar Angus Fletcher says, "necessarily exerts a high degree of control over the way any reader must approach any given work."[33] Any attempt to control interpretation constitutes an insult to creative reading, an insult Nochlin finds not confined to allegory but embedded deep within the premises of the discipline of art history, "in which the production of meaning is all too often foreclosed by restricting its operations to the field of iconography, and within it, to unequivocal interpretations" ("Courbet's Real Allegory," 159). Indeed, as Nochlin ponders the matter, all interpretation comes to seem allegorical insofar as it advances one view at the expense of others. Thoroughly aroused by this time, she rises up not just against an oppressive tendency in her own discipline but against claims of final knowledge in any discipline. She is manifestly and triumphantly delighted to be able to claim as an ally not a theoretician or fellow academic but Courbet himself, who insisted, in an anti-allegorical spirit, that meaning and value are not to be found in some unspecified elsewhere but right here in the world, signaling his own ironic resistance to allegorical closure by leaving his painting unfinished so that his "real allegory" must be read as an allegory of the impossibility of allegory.[34] The real meaning of allegory, properly understood, is not that things have non-obvious but determinate meanings, but that things can have multiple meanings, none definitive: anything can mean anything. Empiricism must yield finally to informed speculation, observed fact to the deeper truth of imaginative construction.

Having swept away allegorical interpretative premises, Nochlin proceeds to engage with the painting not as a schema of determinate meanings but as a "field of uncertainty, in which vague and more substantial incidents rise, assert themselves for a while, and then fade away on the vast projective screen of the canvas" ("Courbet's Real Allegory," 159). Operating now in an open field, Nochlin reclaims a co-creative readerly agency by undertaking to "read as a woman," zeroing in not on the masterly figure of Courbet at the center of the painting but on the huddled, deeply shadowed, almost unnoticeable figure to the left of him. Commonly identified as an Irish beggar woman, this figure seems to cling to precarious life, her misery so particularized that it cannot be reduced to any general meaning such as the plight of Ireland or the sufferings of the poor, and so utter that it cannot be washed away in any general message of peace, harmony, or reconciliation. In "Petites Vieilles," Baudelaire had depicted the poet nursing at the bosom of "austere Misfortune," an image that enables Nochlin to interpolate Courbet himself into the pitiable infant suckling at the breast of the Irish beggar woman, thereby reducing the figure of the artist "from masterful protagonist to almost nothing, a mere nursling beggar" (169). "What could constitute a more devastating response to the intended lesson of Courbet's allegory about the authoritative position of the artist," Nochlin asks, "than this alternative allegorization of the figure of the beggar woman and her almost invisible child?" (170).

Then, claiming for herself one of "the male prerogatives of creativity," Nochlin launches into one of the great moments of scholarly disruption, announcing that she "will now stop reading as a woman and write as one" ("Courbet's Real Allegory," 178). What does that mean? In this case, it means discovering in the painting "another scenario, a real allegory of transgression" in which the central character is not Courbet at all but the nineteenth-century artist Rosa Bonheur, painting not a quiet landscape but a bull (180). It also means seeing the entire composition as a *tableau vivant* in which the painted figures begin to stir. "Suddenly, Champfleury can't stand it any longer. He rises from his seat in the wings and approaches the center. 'But she's not even a *great* artist,' he protests; 'Why are there no great women artists?'" (180). Other figures reveal themselves: Mary Cassatt, Berthe Morisot, Georgia O'Keeffe.

The male figures start to take off their clothes, embracing each other, displaying their buttocks or their "luminous but hairy flesh," reclining on white sheets—in all ways replicating the positions in which painting has placed women (181). The women, observing the men in their ridiculous postures, burst into gales of laughter so violent and protracted that the paint itself begins to melt and flow, resolving finally into pure, dazzling light.

With this carnivalesque finale, Nochlin explodes the closure and finality of allegorical interpretation, which is to say, of interpretation itself. She envisions an anarchically utopian "world upside down" in which all normal relations of domination and hierarchy are overturned. But this is not, she insists, a mere fantasia. Recalling that in the authoritative allegorical reading of the painting, Courbet was presuming to instruct the Emperor, implicitly placing the artist on top, she claims that her own reading, which puts women on top, is entirely faithful to its subject's revolutionary intention.

The peaceable, rule-governed, modest activity of scholarship is not often described as carnivalesque, but the world as comprehended by scholarship is always in process, always provisional, always unfinished, always awaiting the next revolution. In offering a total fiasco as a faithful rendering, Nochlin was following scholarly convention, but doing so to an uncompromised caricatural extreme that lacks the warrant of common sense—a nonscholarly consideration that restrains most scholarly interpretations.

The effects if not the practice of scholarship are actually more radical than Carnival, whose overturnings are ritual, temporary, and licensed by authority, while those of scholarship are unlimited, unpredictable, and (in principle) make no concession to power. Like modernity itself, scholarship implies infinity, an endlessly transformative process in which current understandings are rejected, improved, modified, supplemented, exchanged. The endless quest, the incomplete project, the ongoing conversation, the unresolved debate, the open society—these are the tropes of modernity, which are routinely contrasted to premodern stasis, repetition, and certitude. And so, while Mardi Gras seems a remnant of a distant time, scholarship has a place of privilege in modernity.

The modernity of scholarship is marked most decisively in its reciprocal relation to the concept of human freedom, whose signature, according to Hannah Arendt, is the capacity to create, to begin, to bring something new into the world. Arendt had introduced this thought in a passage at the very end of *The Origins of Totalitarianism* (1948) where, after a sobering and often horrifying historical exploration of antisemitism, racism, imperialism, communism, fascism, and authoritarianism in many forms, she abruptly, and surprisingly to many, alludes to the possibility of a "new beginning" arising from "the supreme capacity of man" to create.[35] Even more surprisingly, she gives the concept a religious as well as a political warrant. "Politically," she says, beginning "is identical with man's freedom. *Initium ut esset homo creatus est*—'that a beginning be made

man was created' said Augustine. This beginning is guar-
anteed by each new birth; it is indeed every man" (479).

What in the world was she thinking?

The concept awaited a fuller elaboration, and a name,
for a decade, until Arendt gave a lecture called "What Is
Freedom?" and published *The Human Condition,* in which
the capacity for beginning was baptized natality.[36] The emphasis on birth as the grounding of human freedom and
creation might be seen as an attempt to depoliticize and
naturalize the human condition. But Arendt's natality is a
biological concept with nonbiological entailments. Like
others at this time, Arendt was looking for a way to place
the moral and political concept of freedom on a firmer
foundation than could be provided by historical traditions
or political institutions, which had proven themselves un-
able to prevent the rise of totalitarianisms. Her effort might
be compared with that of Noam Chomsky, who was at
about the same time training his linguistic and political at-
tentions on the human capacity to generate an infinite
number of new well-formed sentences—evidence, he argued, that human beings were innately "creative," and
therefore that any political order that constrained that creativity was violating not just some notion of justice or
fairness but human nature itself. Both projects represent
attempts to build an antitotalitarian politics of freedom on
a species characteristic. Arendt was arguing that the phe-
nomenon of birth preceded, modeled, and in a sense authorized subsequent creative acts, which could be understood not as risky deviations from routine but as willed

reaffirmations of a natural condition to which every human being bore witness.

The deepest potentialities of natality are realized in what Arendt calls action, one of the three "fundamental activities" that define the human condition, the other two being work and labor. As she says repeatedly, action has a "miraculous" character; and yet true action has nothing to do with religion or faith or the inner life.[37] The abstract terms of *The Human Condition* may seem so capacious that anything at all might qualify as action, but Arendt always insists that freedom is political freedom and action political action: "The *raison d'être* of politics is freedom," she says, "and its field of experience is action" (145). In a final section on "The *Vita Activa* and the Modern Age," Arendt whole-heartedly endorses the modern reversal of the ancient priority of contemplation over action. She dismisses the piffling and evanescent liberties associated with reflection and meditation as shadows of real freedom, as thought is a shadow of action. And she is deeply skeptical, even dis-approving, of attempts to locate a ghostly "inner" freedom, something unknown to the ancient world and peculiar, she points out, to certain forms of Christianity.

Clarity is an excellent thing, but Arendt's prejudice in favor of the political, while understandable considering the postwar context, limits rather than concentrates the power of her thinking. It is hard to see a bright line between inner and outer freedom, especially since Arendt herself insis-tently links action with the language that communicates the action to the world. Action and speech, she says, "are so closely related because the primordial and specifically human act must at the same time contain the answer to the question asked of every newcomer: 'Who are you?'" (*Human Condition*, 178). Without the accompaniment of speech, action might as well be undertaken by robots; complemented by speech, action becomes a testimonial to a unique human individual declaring itself to a community. But speech has deep roots in the inner world of reflection and self-understanding; and stories, to which she devotes an entire section, are implicated in fiction, myth, and unreality in general.

And so we must pose a different question: Is there anything worthy of the name of action that deploys language, that creates something new, that registers human uniqueness, addresses a community, is accountable to reality, and serves the cause of freedom?

The answer, I believe, was right under Arendt's nose; indeed, in many of her other works, it was flowing from her pen. Scholarship is produced by situated individuals exercising personal judgment, it is addressed to an unrestricted public, it follows argumentative procedures that are transparent and transpersonal, and it respects evidence. Scholarship is expressive and communicative, but it is accountable to the world in a way that speech and stories as such are not. Most important, in Arendt's terms, scholarship rejects old understandings and creates new ones. Scholarship is not only, as I said at the beginning, the most refined and disciplined form of the freedoms of inquiry and expression; it stands at the margin of responsible contemplation and informed action. Its mission is not to create a just society or usher in the reign of reason, but to transform the world of death that is the past into something open, something real, something new.

Politics can take it from there.

Conclusion

Too Much Freedom?

THE THIRD MILLENNIUM CE has not been kind to scholarship. The institutions of higher education that once, or so we like to think, organized themselves around the pursuit of knowledge now often seem distracted, conflicted, stressed, or compromised in ways that weaken their commitment to scholarship's methods and goals. The deeply alarming work conditions of faculty, the tendency to intellectual and political conformity on many campuses, the eager dependency of colleges and universities on market forces, and other factors have made it possible to pose a once-unthinkable question, whether colleges and universities truly value scholarship, or even, in some cases, whether they are the right place for scholarship.

To consider these questions as problems specific or exclusive to the academy is, however, to minimize and mischaracterize the situation. Colleges and universities are not the only places where the concept of a form of truth that is difficult to obtain, debatable in its value, and often ambiguous or obscure in its import or utility has lost prestige. In a polarized and locked-down world, conviction often trumps circumspection, and hard-won truth suffers by comparison with hypertrophied opinion, which can be produced and disseminated with greater ease, in greater abundance, by a larger number of people, and to far greater immediate effect than scholarly discourse. Opinions—the elementary particles of social exchange—seem to be increasingly rigid in their content but increasingly loose in the manner in which they are produced and disseminated. At the same time, democratic freedoms, and the social and economic mobility on which democracy is predicated, are being eroded not just in traditionally totalitarian states but in nations with popularly elected governments such as Hungary, Turkey, Israel, the Philippines, the United States, Italy, and Brazil, with significant gains for authoritarian political movements in other countries as well.

One of the arguments of this book is that this is no coincidence, that the fortunes of the necessarily elite practice of scholarship and a more general political and social experience of freedom are if not directly linked at least related, and that they tend to wax and wane together.

Some scholars distribute blame for what they see as a deplorable situation among a list of the usual suspects that includes unregulated technology, social media, extremist politics, and a generally poisoned culture. Others blame scholarship, or at least some scholars. The premise that we live in a "post-truth" world was a shibboleth of the theoretically advanced sectors of the academy before the rise of social media, even before the widespread use of the personal computer. The "social construction" of all principles, facts, and values was a neo-Nietzschean academic banality long before it became an appalling social reality.

Back in that golden afternoon of easy theorizing in the late twentieth century, many of those making such arguments actually felt that they were speaking the truth, and that if people recognized that things long considered natural or simply given were recognized as artifacts of the systems of knowledge and belief that we have ourselves created and could change at will if we wanted to, they would be encouraged to take greater responsibility for their lives. An expanded circumference of human agency, it was believed, would lead to greater confidence in human powers and ultimately to greater opportunities for human self-realization. Scholars would be the honored prophets of this new world. That, at least, was the theory.

In practice, however, the post-truth era has not seen a world pliant to our desires, but rather a world of diminished social and economic mobility, and increasing cultural and intellectual rigidity. On bad days, it can seem like a world in which nothing can change except to become more so. When questions are decided in advance by identifications or affiliations, no broad consensus seems possible on any issue regardless of the evidence, because nothing has the force necessary to overpower entrenched opinion. And when opinion is divided, nothing advances or progresses.

None of the three scholars discussed at length in the preceding pages could have done what they did in a culture where scholarship was devalued. Each one faced at some point in his or her career an opposing edifice of conviction, and each deployed the instruments of scholarship in the service of an emancipatory agenda. Scholarship was suited to this task because it had, in the communities they were addressing and hoped to influence, great prestige and authority. In these communities, it was generally believed that scholarship favored no party, that it was neutral with respect to ideologies and values, and that it was therefore the best and fairest method of determining a reality in which everyone had a share.

Scholarship conceived in these terms is implicitly hostile to the status quo and threatening to those who seek to maintain it. The activity of returning to the past in a spirit of skepticism, disinterest, and openness to the evidence whatever it might say can only jeopardize and alienate those whose position depends upon maintaining currently accepted truths. Scholarship's inbuilt challenge to power is a deeply attractive feature to many scholars because it suggests that scholars stand in a privileged position outside the circle of illusion that functions for others as received wisdom or common sense.

The most heroic accounts of scholarship carry the implication that the scholar is the one honest person in town, a solitary but righteous figure whose only ally—but that the most formidable possible—is the truth. Near the end of his witty and lighthearted "curious history" of the footnote, Anthony Grafton makes the striking statement that "only the use of footnotes and the research techniques associated with them makes it possible to resist the efforts of modern governments, tyrannical and democratic alike, to conceal the compromises they have made, the deaths they have caused, the tortures they or their allies have inflicted."[1] For some reason, Grafton does not pursue this line of thought beyond that arresting sentence, but perhaps he feels he does not need to, because for scholars—and who else will read a book on the footnote?—the case is self-evident: scholars are singularly well equipped to undermine the mythical or ideologically driven accounts of the past and present that support the powers that be, and to clear the ground for a better set of arrangements based on the truth.

Scholars sometimes claim that they welcome the hatred of power (unless they are actually fired, silenced, jailed, or worse) because they see in that hatred a sign of fear. In the story scholars sometimes tell themselves, autocrats and authoritarians fear the footnote because they fear the open, liberal society that would ultimately result from a scholarly inquiry into the truth. Tyrants fear being outlived by footnotes, as larger and more imposing species may be outlasted and eventually consumed by roaches, ants, and microbes—in fact, scholars say with no small measure of satisfaction, tyrants fear becoming footnotes themselves in a world where scholarship, but not despotism, flourishes.

But this may overstate the case for the scholar's commitment to openness and neutrality, for scholars are never altogether disinterested or indifferent to power. The everyday struggle of the scholar concerns not tyranny and injustice but received ideas, and here the record is less heroic and more equivocal. For while scholars invariably seek to overturn current knowledge, they just as insistently try to put better knowledge in its place, and to defend their work against objections so that their ideas will become "received." Their defenses often reveal extra-scholarly commitments, which of course they have like everyone else. Scholarship, to borrow a phrase from Linda Nochlin, is the activity of "a subject in a situation"; or rather, it is one particular activity undertaken by an individual subject in a certain situation. No scholar is only a scholar. All live in the world, all have interests, responsibilities, desires, concerns, affiliations, roles, and identifications. They are happiest when the truth revealed by their scholarship accords with their values and convictions. They have what in other contexts would be called a conflict of interest, a conflict created by the presence of interest itself in a domain supposedly governed by disinterestedness.

We can test this proposition by performing a thought experiment. If Du Bois had discovered, in his study of Reconstruction, that African Americans during this period were generally lazy, ignorant, irresponsible, corrupt, and unsuited for democracy, would he have trumpeted his results to the world with the same angry defiance as he did in the book he actually wrote? If Lategan had returned to Paul's Letter to the Galatians after the end of the apartheid regime, and discovered to his dismay that the apartheid reading was in fact the hermeneutically correct one, would

he have issued a pained retraction and joined the revanchist opposition? If Nochlin, a boldly interdisciplinary
scholar, had become convinced by research in other fields
that women were not socially but genetically disadvan-
taged when it came to great achievement in the arts,
would she have written a witty and pungent essay that
sought to de-found the field of feminist art history that she
had founded?

Of course not. For each one of these scholars, one
revolution—or rather, half a revolution, 180 degrees—
was enough. Scholarship for them was a weapon wielded
in the service of ends that scholarship had no share in
determining.

This is undoubtedly a good thing, for who would choose
to live in a world in which the premises and practices of
scholarship had an unquestioned priority? Would anyone
think the world would be improved if detachment and neutrality became normative? In which *que sera sera* was the
law of the land? In which, as Marx said in the first chapter
of *The Communist Manifesto,* "all that is solid melts into air,"
and everything, beginning with the "modes of production," was held to be temporary and provisional, awaiting
the moment when it would yield the stage to its unknown
successor?

And yet this would be the world under the unchallenged
reign of scholarship. The truth will set you free, but it may
set you free from things you wish to trust and believe in.
Committed to its own emancipatory agenda, scholarship
seeks liberation not just from the easy targets of dogma,
prejudice, and myth, but from anything that is currently

known or assumed. It is radical—uncompromising, relentless, corrosive, extreme—only on its own behalf, and indifferent to the worldly consequences. It is right, then, that scholarship should take its place among other modes of thought more accepting of the consolations of solidity, more respectful of the comforts of repetition, more accommodating to the need to believe and trust, and more sensitive to the real-time needs of actual people.

Scholarship is not a solution to all problems, a model for knowledge in general, the apex of cognition, or the royal road to reality. It is, however, an indispensable instrument by which people in a modern world can detach themselves from the current moment, revisiting the past in order to understand the present differently, thereby creating the possibility for a different future. It offers people the vision of a world perfectly real—confirmed by documentary evidence—and yet entirely beyond their senses, interests, and desires; a world held in common and in which everyone has a share; a world both dead and buried and yet pregnant with possibility.

NOTES

ACKNOWLEDGMENTS

INDEX

NOTES

1. "Are we animals?," comment recorded by W. E. B. Du Bois in *The Autobiography of W. E. B. Du Bois: A Soliloquy on Viewing My Life from the Last Decade of Its First Century*, in Henry Louis Gates Jr., *The Oxford W. E. B. Du Bois* (New York: Oxford University Press, 2007; orig. pub. 1968), 124. Hereafter *Autobiography*. Other quotations are from W. E. B. Du Bois, *The Philadelphia Negro: A Social Study*, in *The Oxford W. E. B. Du Bois*, ed. Henry Louis Gates Jr. (New York: Oxford University Press, 1986; orig. pub. 1899). "tinsel and braggadocio," 161; "Lombard Street," 198; "certain peculiar social problems," 3. Du Bois was particularly offended by Seventh Ward spending habits. Listing figures for wages, rent, and expenditures for ten sample families, he notes that "the meat bill of the average Negro family would surprise a French or German peasant or even an Englishman. The crowds that line Lombard street on Sundays are dressed far beyond their means; much money is wasted in extravagantly furnished parlors, dining-rooms. . . . Thousands of dollars are annually wasted in excessive rents, in doubtful

'societies' of all kinds, in amusements of various kinds, and in miscellaneous ornaments and gewgaws. . . . The Negro has much to learn of the Jew and Italian, as to living within his means and saving every penny from excessive and wasteful expenditures." *Philadelphia Negro*, 127, 128.

2. W. E. B. Du Bois, *The Souls of Black Folk*, in *W. E. B. Du Bois: Writings*, ed. Nathan Huggins (New York: Library of America, 1986), 357–546. Orig. pub. 1903. Hereafter *Souls*.

3. In *Dusk of Dawn*, Du Bois downplays the racial slight of the visiting card incident, and notes that "the racial angle was more clearly defined against the Irish than against me." W. E. B. Du Bois, *Dusk of Dawn: An Essay toward an Autobiography of a Race Concept*, in Huggins, *W. E. B. Du Bois: Writings*, 549–802, 563. Orig. pub. 1940.

4. Henry Louis Gates Jr., "The Black Letters on the Sign: W. E. B. Du Bois and the Canon," in Du Bois, *Philadelphia Negro*, xiv.

5. Sean Wilentz, *The Politicians and the Egalitarians: The Hidden History of American Politics* (New York: W. W. Norton, 2016), 260.

6. Du Bois popularized but did not invent the phrase "talented tenth." See W. E. B. Du Bois, "The Talented Tenth," in *The Negro Problem: A Series of Articles by Representative American Negroes of Today*, ed. Booker T. Washington (New York: J. J. Pott, 1903), 31–76.

7. W. E. Burghardt Du Bois, *Darkwater: Voices from within the Veil* (New York: Harcourt, Brace and Howe, 1920), 14.

8. For the argument that education rather than industrial training was the optimal course for black men, see also Du Bois, "Of Mr. Booker T. Washington and Others," in *Souls*,

392–404; and "Of the Training of Black Men," in *Souls,* 424–38.

9. W. E. B. Du Bois, "The Afro-American," in *The Problem of the Color-Line at the Turn of the Twentieth Century,* ed. Nahum Dimitri Chandler (New York: Fordham University Press, 2015), 33–50, 46.

10. John Hope Franklin, *Mirror to America: The Autobiography of John Hope Franklin* (New York: Farrar, Straus and Giroux, 2005), 117.

11. So preeminent was Berlin in the world of scholarship that the university did not even recognize a degree from Harvard. As Du Bois puts it, Berlin was to Harvard as Harvard was to Fisk. See Du Bois, *Autobiography, 99.* The university counted among its alumni and faculty Johann Gottlieb Fichte (rector 1810–1812), G. W. F. Hegel (rector 1830–1831), both Grimm brothers, Theodor Mommsen, Max Planck, Georg Simmel, Ernst Curtius, and Ulrich von Wilamovitz-Moellendorff.

12. Peter Novick, *That Noble Dream: The "Objectivity Question" and the American Historical Profession* (Cambridge: Cambridge University Press, 1988), 31.

13. In his study of the profession of scholarship in the popular imagination, A. D. Nuttall comments that the concept of "trying to get *everything* right involves a queer, abstract *altruism of the intellect* and it took thousands of years to learn." On the concept of "comprehensive" knowledge, Nuttall adds that scholarship "connotes a quality of completeness," beginning with perfect accuracy and extending to "a broad front of total accuracy, a sort of democracy of fact, in which no atom of truth shall be slighted, however

humble in relation to the main theme." Nuttall, *Dead from the Waist Down: Scholars and Scholarship in Literature and the Popular Imagination* (New Haven, CT: Yale University Press, 2011), 191.

14. The student, Herman Nohl, is quoted in Ramon J. Betanzos, "Wilhelm Dilthey: An Introduction," in Wilhelm Dilthey, *Introduction to the Human Sciences: An Attempt to Lay a Foundation for the Study of Society and History*, trans. Ramon J. Betanzos (Detroit: Wayne State University Press, 1988), 9–65, 10. The comment on the identity of Dilthey and his work is made by Betanzos, 10.

15. Leopold von Ranke, *History of the Reformation in Germany*, ed. Robert A. Johnson, trans. Sarah Austin (London: George Routledge and Sons, 1905), ix. Orig. pub. 1854–1857.

16. This understanding has long been held against Ranke, who has been charged with naïve or even mindless empiricism. But Richard Evans argues that the phrase should actually be translated "how it essentially was," which leaves open the possibility for a more speculative approach that would proceed from general ideas of the sort that a thoroughgoing commitment to empiricism would seem to rule out. Evans, *In Defence of History* (London: Granta Books, 2000), 17. Novick makes a similar point in *That Noble Dream*, 28.

17. Du Bois seminar notes, quoted in Francis L. Broderick, "German Influence on the Scholarship of W. E. B. Du Bois," *Phylon* 19 (December 1958): 367–71, 369.

18. W. E. B. Du Bois, *The Suppression of the African Slave-Trade*, in Huggins, *W. E. B. Du Bois: Writings*. Orig. pub. 1896.

19. Roger Lane calls *The Philadelphia Negro* the "best piece of sociology written by an American in the nineteenth

century." Lane, *Roots of Violence in Black Philadelphia, 1860–1900* (Cambridge, MA: Harvard University Press, 1986), 148. The strongest claims for the book as a pioneering document in the development of scientific sociology are made by Aldon D. Morris in *The Scholar Denied: W. E. B Du Bois and the Birth of Modern Sociology* (Berkeley: University of California Press, 2015). Morris argues that only an endemic racism, coupled with a disciplinary conservatism, among sociologists has prevented a fair assessment of Du Bois's originality. For an excellent discussion of *The Philadelphia Negro*, see David Levering Lewis, *W. E. B. Du Bois: Biography of a Race, 1868–1919*, 2 vols. (New York: Henry Holt, 1993), 1:201–10.

20. On the Atlanta University Studies publications that grew out of these conferences, see Lewis, *W. E. B. Du Bois*, 1:217–25, 346–52.

21. Heinrich von Treitschke, *Politik: Vorlesungen gehalten an der Universität zu Berlin* (Leipzig: Verlag von Hirzel, 1899), translated and quoted in Kwame Anthony Appiah, *Lines of Descent: W. E. B. Du Bois and the Emergence of Identity* (Cambridge, MA: Harvard University Press, 2014), 69. Appiah notes that this pronouncement would have resonated with Du Bois, whose 1897 Negro Academy address supposed that "200,000,000 black hearts beating in one glad song of jubilee" were required for the Negro to achieve full historical agency (69).

22. Erich Auerbach, *Mimesis: The Representation of Reality in Western Literature*, trans. Willard R. Trask, intro. by Edward Said (Princeton, NJ: Princeton University Press, 2003), 548, 549. With the passage of time, the urgent historical and

political determinants of Auerbach's magisterial work have become clearer, and it has become possible to read both his great essay "Figura" and the monumental *Mimesis* as instruments of a personal Kulturkampf against the premises not just of German philology but of the barbarism of the Third Reich. See on this point Avihu Zakai, *Erich Auerbach and the Crisis of German Philology: The Humanist Tradition in Peril* (Dordrecht: Springer, 2016). The salient point in the present context is that no matter how gravely stressed and fearful Auerbach may have been, he chose scholarship as his medium of resistance and counterattack.

23. Wilhelm von Humboldt, "On Germany's Educational System," in *The Rise of the Research University: A Sourcebook,* ed. Louis Menand, Paul Reitter, and Chad Wellmon (Chicago: University of Chicago Press, 2017), 108–16, 109.

24. Hearing this text read in a church, the man who would become St. Antony followed its instructions (and gave his sister to a convent) and left the city, eventually making his way to a walled-in tomb in the Egyptian desert, where he experienced the temptations documented so vividly by Athanasius in *The Life of Antony* (c. 360). For preliminary reflections on the connection between ascesis and scholarship, see Geoffrey Galt Harpham, "The Ascetics of Interpretation," in *The Ascetic Imperative in Culture and Criticism* (Chicago: University of Chicago Press, 1987), 237–70.

25. Peter Brown, "The Rise and Function of the Holy Man in Late Antiquity," *Journal of Roman Studies* 61 (1971): 80–101.

26. See Appiah, *Lines of Descent,* 29–31. As Novick says, Ranke's politics amounted to a neo-Hegelian "pantheistic state-worship" (*That Noble Dream,* 27). And as Lionel Gossman

reports, Ranke's student Heinrich von Sybel described himself as "four sevenths politician and three sevenths professor." Gossman, *Between History and Literature* (Cambridge, MA: Harvard University Press, 1990), 83. Gossman also details the extensive political involvements of French Romantic historians, particularly Augustin Thierry, in chapter 4, "Thierry and Liberal Historiography," 83–151.

27. Nuttall, *Dead from the Waist Down*, x. Nuttall continues in this passage to note that "within the academy, however, among the intellectuals themselves, there has been a paradoxical rejection of the notion of cold intellectual neutrality . . . and a sudden obsession with sexuality" (x).

28. "fire-eating pan-German," Du Bois, *Dusk of Dawn*, 588; "German Machiavelli," Du Bois, *Autobiography*, 103; "volcanic bigot," Lewis, *W. E. B. Du Bois*, 1:136.

29. Max Weber, "Methods of Social Science," in *From Max Weber: Essays in Sociology*, trans. H. H. Gerth (New York: Routledge, 2007; orig. pub. 1947), 55–60, 58.

30. "morally reprehensible forms of trade," Gustav von Schmoller, "The Social Question," quoted in Appiah, *Lines of Descent*, 33; "moral duty," Schmoller, quoted in Nicholas Balabkins, *Not by Theory Alone . . . : The Economics of Gustav von Schmoller and Its Legacy to America* (Berlin: Duncker & Humblot, 1988), 41. By their nature, opinions are exposed to the charge that they reflect ideas personal to the scholar. A. D. Nuttall says, "I fancy that it would take little labour to show that high scholarship is compatible with prejudice and bigotry carried to extremes"; Nuttall, *Dead from the Waist Down*, 199.

31. Du Bois, *Autobiography*, 104.

32. Novick cites the findings of a sociologist who compared the workplace behavior at an advertising agency with that of a university faculty, finding that the admen behaved better. Why? "The sociologist's hypothesis was that those in advertising, nagged by guilt about their social product, felt obliged to expiate their sins by being nice to their colleagues. The academics, overwhelmed with the transcendent moral worth of their activity, believed that on that account they had a plenary indulgence to act badly." Novick, *That Noble Dream,* 15–16.

33. Ranke, *History of the Reformation,* xi.

34. On the racial views of Du Bois's professors, see Appiah, *Lines of Descent,* 83–100.

35. Wilhelm Dilthey, "The Rise of Hermeneutics," trans. Fredric Jameson, *New Literary History* 3, no. 2 (Winter 1972; orig. pub. 1900): 229–44, 230. See also Dilthey, *Introduction to the Human Sciences.* In *Objectivity,* Peter Galison and Lorraine Daston demonstrate that in the eighteenth century, the English word "objective" referred to the sense of things as presented to the senses, while "subjective" referred to the apprehension of things in themselves—the opposite of the usage that came to dominate in the mid-nineteenth century and since. Peter Galison and Lorraine Daston, *Objectivity* (Brooklyn: Zone Books, 2007), 29.

36. On Dilthey's emphasis on narrative, see Jos de Mul, "Dilthey's Narrative Model of Human Development: Necessary Reconsiderations after the Philosophical Hermeneutics of Heidegger and Gadamer," *Man and World* 24 (1991): 409–26; and Jacob Owensby, *Dilthey and the Narrative of History* (Ithaca, NY: Cornell University Press, 1994).

37. Gossman, *Between History and Literature*, 291–93.

38. Lester Frank Ward, *Pure Sociology: A Treatise on the Origin and Spontaneous Development of Society*, 2nd ed. (New York: Macmillan, 1907; orig. pub. 1903), 99.

39. Gossman, *Between History and Literature*, 292.

40. As Ramon J. Betanzos writes, Dilthey's work has the character of a series of beginnings or preliminary sketches, announcements of something to come. He is, Betanzos notes, known as the "man of the half-volume" and "the great fragmentist" whose work "is widely regarded as merely *transitional*, as leading to later, more substantial, philosophies and systems." Betanzos, "Wilhelm Dilthey: An Introduction," in Dilthey, *Introduction to the Human Sciences*, 11.

41. Du Bois, *Philadelphia Negro*, 243.

42. Edward Said, *Orientalism*, 2nd ed. (New York: Vintage Books, 1994), 132.

43. Kelly Miller, "Radicals and Conservatives," in *Race Adjustment: Essays on the Negro in America*, 2nd ed. (New York: Neale Publishing, 1909), 11–27, 15.

44. "How else," White wrote, "can any past, which by definition comprises events, processes, structures, and so forth, considered to be no longer perceivable, be represented in either consciousness or discourse except in an 'imaginary' way?" Hayden White, "Narrative in Contemporary Historical Theory," in *The Content of the Form: Narrative Discourse and Historical Representation* (Baltimore: Johns Hopkins University Press, 1987), 26–57, 57. See also Hayden White, *Metahistory: The Historical Imagination in Nineteenth-Century Europe* (Baltimore: Johns Hopkins University Press, 1973); and Paul Ricoeur, *Time and Narrative*, 2 vols. (Chicago: University of

Chicago Press, 1984). On the debate among historians about the status of narrative, see Lawrence Stone, "The Revival of Narrative," *Past and Present* 85 (November 1979): 3–24.

45. Novick, *That Noble Dream*, 573–629.

46. Interview quoted by Lewis, *W. E. B. Du Bois*, 1:226.

47. W. E. B. Du Bois, *Black Reconstruction in America: An Essay toward a History of the Part which Black Folk Played in the Attempt to Reconstruct Democracy in America, 1860–1880* (New York: Oxford University Press, 2007; orig. pub. 1935).

48. The essay begins, "Joseph Stalin was a great man; few other men of the twentieth century approach his stature," and ends by rebuking the "noisy jackals and ill-bred men of some parts of the distempered West" who think differently. W. E. B. Du Bois, "On Stalin," *National Guardian* (16 March 1953), https://www.marxists.org/reference/archive /stalin/biographies/1953/03/16.htm, accessed 14 July 2018.

2. CONVERSION AND THE QUESTION OF EVIDENCE

1. Leopold von Ranke, *History of the Reformation in Germany*, ed. Robert A. Johnson, trans. Sarah Austin (London: George Routledge and Sons, 1905), xi. Orig. pub. 1854–1857. Ranke was not the only historian to place an almost unlimited trust in eyewitness accounts. Lionel Gossman quotes the words of Prosper de Barante, writing in the preface to *Histoire des Ducs de Bourgoogne* (1824) in praise of the Old French chroniclers, who "always know how to make us see [events] exactly as they appeared before their own eyes" (cited in Lionel Gossman, *Between History and Literature*

[Cambridge, MA: Harvard University Press, 1990], 118). As Gossman points out, however, Barante's efforts to disguise his own role as writer and to attribute his conclusions to the evidence provided by documents make his history "if anything, more ideologically loaded" (121).

2. For an account of the speculative character of much philological research especially in the nineteenth century, see Geoffrey Galt Harpham, "Roots, Races, and the Return to Philology," in *The Humanities and the Dream of America* (Chicago: University of Chicago Press, 2011), 43–79.

3. See Lorenzo Valla, *On the Donation of Constantine,* trans. G. W. Bowersock (Cambridge, MA: Harvard University Press, 2007). Bowersock notes that this text "has often been seen, rightly, as the beginning of serious philological criticism" (vii). Sadly, modern scholarship only rarely reaches the heights of righteous scholarly indignation achieved by Valla. Pointing out the anachronism in one word in the Donation of Constantine, Valla challenges an imagined opponent in splendid vernacular Latin, which Bowersock renders as "You scoundrel, you miscreant. . . . Why do you want to bring in *satraps*? You blockhead, you dolt! Do emperors talk that way?" (67).

4. Erwin Panofsky, "The History of Art as a Humanistic Discipline," in *Meaning in the Visual Arts* (Chicago: University of Chicago Press, 1955; orig. pub. 1939), 1–25, 5.

5. In a 2016 article, John Guillory deploys Panofsky's document-monument distinction to argue for a "new conception of the humanistic object," the document-monument axis. See John Guillory, "Monuments and Documents: Panofsky on

the Object of Study in the Humanities," *History of Humanities*
1, no. 1 (2016): 9–30. For a response that points out that this
"object" remains subjective, see Geoffrey Galt Harpham,
"Response to John Guillory," *History of Humanities* 1, no. 1
(2016): 41–45.

6. This distinction has, of course, long been questioned. To
take only one example of such questioning, Hans Albert
writes that scientific cognition is "shot through with regu-
lations, valuations, and decisions. . . . We choose our problems, evaluate solutions to them, and decide to prefer one
of the available solutions to others." Hans Albert, *Treatise
on Critical Reason,* trans. Mary Varney Rorty (Princeton, NJ:
Princeton University Press, 1985), 100.

7. E. H. Carr, *What Is History?* (New York: Vintage Books,
1961). Objectivity has been the subject of three extraordinary books: Thomas Haskell, *Objectivity Is Not Neutrality:
Explanatory Schemes in History* (Baltimore: Johns Hopkins
University Press, 1998); Peter Novick, *That Noble Dream: The
"Objectivity Question" and the American Historical Profession*
(Cambridge: Cambridge University Press, 1988); and, for an
account centering on science rather than history, Peter Galison and Lorraine Daston, *Objectivity* (Brooklyn: Zone
Books, 2007). All three identify deep historical roots to the
concept, with a particularly important precursor discipline
in Baconian science, but locate its full emergence in the
early nineteenth century.

8. Paul Valéry, "Historical Fact," in *History and Politics,*
trans. Denise Folliot and Jackson Mathews, vol. 10 of *Col-
lected Works of Paul Valéry* (Princeton, NJ: Princeton University Press, 1971), 69.

9. Hugh Trevor-Roper, introduction to Jacob Burckhardt, *Burckhardt: Judgements on History and Historians,* trans. Harry Zohn (New York: Routledge, 1959), xii–xxiv, xxii.

10. Peter Brown, *The Body and Society: Men, Women, and Sexual Renunciation in Early Christianity* (New York: Columbia University Press, 1998), 446–47.

11. Stephen Greenblatt, *Shakespearean Negotiations: The Circulation of Social Energy in Renaissance England* (Berkeley: University of California Press, 1988). Speaking with the dead is not only a "familiar motive" in literary studies, but has a much longer genealogy in the history of learning. As he was writing *The Prince,* Machiavelli wrote to Francesco Vettori, describing his life. After a day of catching thrushes barehanded, conversing with woodsmen, and playing backgammon, he says, "I return home and enter my study; on the threshold I take off my workday clothes, covered with mud and dirt, and put on the garments of court and palace. Fitted out appropriately, I step inside the venerable courts of the ancients, where, solicitously received by them, I nourish myself on that food that alone is mine and for which I was born; where I am unashamed to converse with them and to question them about the motives for their actions, and they, out of their human kindness, answer me . . . I absorb myself into them completely." Niccolò Machiavelli, letter to Francesco Vettori, 10 December 1513, in *Machiavelli and His Friends: Their Personal Correspondence,* trans. and ed. J. B. Atkinson and David Sices (De Kalb: Northern Illinois University Press, 1996), 264.

12. As Greenblatt says, the notion of the "text itself" as the stable site of evidence of Shakespeare's original intentions

has been so persuasively debunked by textual and theater historians that it is now simply impossible to take the text as the "perfect, unsubstitutable, freestanding container of all of its meanings" (3).

13. Max Weber, "Science as a Vocation," in *The Vocation Lectures*, trans. Rodney Livingston, ed. David Owen and Tracy B. Strong (Indianapolis: Hackett Publishing, 2004).

14. Lionel Gossman provides an example from his own career that illuminates this point. He had, he says, developed a theory whose flaws he did not recognize "for reasons I suspect were closely connected with my own personality and my own general feeling of political disillusionment." One day, the historian Carl Schorske attended Gossman's seminar, and casually proposed a theory "totally at odds" with the one Gossman had held. "I don't think a physical blow would have wounded me more," he says (308). After an immense amount of penitential reading, Gossman realized that Schorske was right. He attributed this change of heart to his improved understanding of the evidence alone, but included this anecdote in the course of a discourse titled "History as Product and Process" that poses the question of why and how scholars change their minds. Clearly, Gossman felt that in renouncing his own view—and confessing to personal failings that were responsible for those views—and converting to Schorske's view, he was exercising the right kind of freedom, demonstrating an admirably modest capacity for submission to the evidence, as well as an appropriately deferential respect for the distinguished Schorske. Gossman, *History and Literature*, 307–17, 308.

15. Steven Toulmin argues that scientific and, a fortiori, scholarly fields are transmitted not in the form of doctrines but rather in the form of skills and methods in a process of *"enculturation."* This, for Toulmin, is not the opposite of rationality but its very criterion: "We judge the rationality of a man's conduct by considering, not how he habitually behaves, but rather how far he modified his behavior in new and unfamiliar situations . . . by the manner in which he modified [his] intellectual position in the face of new and unforeseen experiences." Toulmin, *Human Understanding: The Collective Use and Evolution of Concepts* (Princeton, NJ: Princeton University Press, 1972), 486.

16. https://fabryhistory.com/2015/05/11/apartheid-a-policy-of -good-neighborliness/. Verwoerd, a former psychologist and sociologist at Stellenbosch University, was speaking at a time when millions of black people were being removed from their homes and resettled in either Soweto on the outskirts of Johannesburg or in one of ten designated "tribal homelands," or Bantustans.

17. In 1974, the Dutch Reformed Church issued a statement entitled, in English, *Human Relations and the South African Scene in the Light of Scripture* that defined the Church's role as one of "reconciliation," while insisting that respect for "sphere sovereignty" and racial separation was Biblically ordained (Afrikaans version published 1974, Dutch Reformed Church).

18. By "everyone of importance," I do not mean everyone of significance, only those who held the reins of power. There were other Afrikaners who, for various reasons, were not part of "Afrikaner society" in this respect. The family

of John Coetzee, for example, was of Dutch descent, had been in Africa since the seventeenth century, spoke Afrikaans, and were nominal members of a Calvinist church; but they and others saw themselves as subjects of the British Crown, to which they remained loyal even during the Boer War of 1899–1902. As the nationalist movement gathered force in the 1930s and 1940s, the concept of the Afrikaner became increasingly militant and ideological, and such people found themselves on the outside of "Afrikaner society."

19. H. Russel Botman, "The Church Partitioned or the Church Reconciled," in *Race and Reconciliation in South Africa: A Multicultural Dialogue in Comparative Perspective,* ed. William E. Van Vugt and G. Daan Cloete (Lanham, MD: Lexington Books, 2000), 107.

20. W. Nicol, "'n Grootse roeping," in *Regverdige Rasse-Apartheid,* ed. G. Cronjé, W. Nicol, and E. P. Groenewald (Stellenbosch: CSV maatskappy van Suid-afrika, 1947), 21–22. Translated in Rothney S. Tshaka, *Confessional Theology: A Critical Analysis of the Theology of Karl Barth* (Newcastle: Cambridge Scholars Publishing, 2010), 198.

21. See, for example, Bernard C. Lategan, "'For Some Useful Purpose' (1 Cor. 12:7)—a Pauline Perspective on the Unity and Diversity in the Church," *RES Theological Bulletin* 4 (1976): 1–9. On Lategan's career, see Cilliers Breytenbach, "'Not according to Human Criteria': Bernard Lategan's Reading of Galatians in a Crumbling *Apartheid* State," in *The New Testament Interpreted: Essays in Honor of Bernard C. Lategan,* ed. Cilliers Breytenbach, Johan C. Thom, and Jeremy Punt (Leiden: Brill, 2006), 53–67. The most lucid and direct account of Lategan's transformation is, unsurprisingly, Bernard C.

Lategan, "Reading the Letter to the Galatians from an *Apart-heid* and a Post-*Apartheid* Perspective," in *The Personal Voice in Biblical Interpretation,* ed. Ingrid Rosa Kitzberger (London: Routledge, 1999), 128–41, 132–33; and Botman, "Church Partitioned," 109.

22. Lategan, "Reading the Letter to the Galatians," 132. For an efficient overview of the relations between the Dutch Reformed Church and the South African apartheid state, see Johann van der Merwe, "The Dutch Reformed Church from *Human Relations and the South African Scene in the Light of Scripture* to *Church and Society:* The Struggle Goes On," *Studia Historiae Ecclesiasticae* 39, no. 1 (May 2013), http://www.scielo.org.za/scielo.php?script=sci_arttext&pid=S1017-04992013000100010, accessed 15 September 2018. See also J. A. Loubser, *The Apartheid Bible: A Critical Review of Racial Theology in South Africa* (Cape Town, South Africa: Maskew Miller Longman, 1987); John de Gruchy, *The Church Struggle in South Africa* (Eugene, OR: Wipf and Stock, 1979); John de Gruchy, *Bonhoeffer and South Africa: Theology and Dialogue* (Grand Rapids, MI: W. B. Eerdmans Publishing, 1984); W. A. de Klerk, *The Puritans in Africa: A Story of Afrikanerdom* (New York: Penguin, 1976); and Johann Kinghorn, "The Theology of Separate Equality: A Critical Outline of the DRC's Position on Apartheid," in *Christianity amidst Apartheid: Selected Perspectives on the Church in South Africa,* ed. Martin Proz-esky (London: Macmillan, 1990), 57–80. This volume represents an excellent selection of perspectives from the crucial years of the late 1980s.

23. Liberation movements often practice their own forms of discrimination. Among the American examples are the

abolitionist movement of the antebellum period, in which women (including Elizabeth Cady Stanton and Lucretia Mott) struggled to find a place; the women's rights movement founded by Stanton and Mott, in which black women found little support; the women's suffrage movement led by Stanton and Susan B. Anthony, in which black women were marginalized; and the Black Power movement of the 1960s, which was explicitly based on an aggressive vision of black manhood.

24. For the apartheid use of this passage, see Winsome Munro, "Romans 13:1–7 Apartheid's Last Biblical Refuge," *Biblical Theology Bulletin: Journal of Bible and Culture* 20 (1990) 4: 161–68. See also Lategan, "Reading Romans 13 in a South African Context," in *Hermeneutics and Social Transformation: A Selection from the Essays of Bernard C. Lategan,* ed. Dirk J. Smit (Stellenbosch: Sun Press, 2015), 65–78. See also Elelwani B. Farisani, "Interpreting the Bible in the Context of Apartheid and Beyond: An African Perspective," *Studia Historiae Ecclesiasticae* 40, no. 2 (2014), http://www.scielo.org.za /scielo.php?script=sci_arttext&pid=S1017-04992014000 300014. For an overview of the American uses of Romans 13, see Lincoln Mullen, "The Fight to Define Romans 13," *The Atlantic,* 15 June 2018, https://www.theatlantic.com/politics /archive/2018/06/romans-13/562916/. This verse has often been used in a context of repression and reaction, but Mullen concludes his discussion by noting that elsewhere in Romans, Paul sums up God's laws "in this word, 'Love your neighbor as yourself.'" For a brief overview of the vast quantities of American scholarship that supported racist premises, see Donald Yacavone, "'Textbook Racism," *Chronicle*

Review, 8 April 2018, https://www.chronicle.com/article/How
-Scholars-Sustained-White/243053?cid=trend_right_a.

25. James Chandler, Arnold I. Davidson, and Harry Harootunian, introduction to *Questions of Evidence: Proof, Practice,
and Persuasion across the Disciplines,* ed. James Chandler, Arnold I. Davidson, and Harry Harootunian (Chicago: University of Chicago Press, 1994), 1–8, 2. The material was
gathered from issues of *Critical Inquiry* from 1991 to 1993.

26. The focus on Lategan in what follows necessarily reduces
an exceptionally complicated history to a narrative about
an individual. But Lategan was not the earliest, or the most
effective, or the most heroic of DRC critics of apartheid. A
fuller account would begin with Beyers Naudé, whose remarkable career is alluded to below.

27. Van der Merwe, "The Dutch Reformed Church," cites this
statement as *Handelinge van die Algemene Sinode van die Nederduitsch Gereformeerde Sendingkerk* (1982), 602. Lategan
left the University of the Western Cape for Stellenbosch in
large part, he has said, to create the possibility of the first
nonwhite faculty appointment there, a hope that was realized when Daan Cloete was hired to replace him.

28. Issued as "Challenge to the Church: A Theological Comment on the Political Crisis in South Africa," https://web
.archive.org/web/20110421034051/ and http://www.sahistory
.org.za/pages/library-resources/officialdocs/kairos-document
.htm.

29. Quoted in F. M. Gaum, *Die verhaal van die Ned Geref Kerk
se Reis Met Apartheid* [The story of the Dutch Reformed
Church's journey with apartheid] (Wellington: Boland,
1997), 18; translated and cited in Van der Merwe, "The Dutch

Reformed Church." In 1990, a General Synod of the DRC met, its schismatic co-religionists now no longer part of the main body of the Church, and issued a statement that reaffirmed opposition to apartheid and confessed to the errors in scholarship that had led to their previous support. The Church, the Synod states, had considered apartheid "too abstractly, and therefore too uncritically"; it had mistakenly allowed forced separation of people "to be considered a biblical narrative"; any such system, they now said, is deemed "unacceptable in the Light of Scripture" and "in conflict with the Bible." *Kerk en Samelewing* [*Church and Society*], in "'n Getuienis van die Nederduitsch Gereformeerde Kerk" (Bloemfontein: NG Sendingpers, 1990), 39–40; cited and translated in van der Merwe, "The Dutch Reformed Church." For a very detailed account of the events surrounding the Belhar Confession, see Mary-Ann Plaatjies van Huffel, "The Belhar Confession: Born in the Struggle against Apartheid in Southern Africa," *Studia Historiae Ecclesiasticae* 39, no. 1 (May 2013): 1–11.

30.   Bernard C. Lategan, "Current Issues in the Hermeneutical Debate," in Smit, *Hermeneutics and Social Transformation*, 13–27, 19; originally published in *Neotestamentica* 18 (1984): 1–17.

31.   "one of the most . . . ," D. J. Smit, "A Reader's Reception of Lategan's Legacy," in Breytenbach, Thom, and Punt, *The New Testament Interpreted*, 3–25, 7; "ruling conventions of exegesis . . . ," Lategan, "Current Issues," 19.

32.   Bernard C. Lategan, E. de Villiers, L. M. du Plessis, and J. Kinghorn, *The Option for Inclusive Democracy* (Stellenbosch: Centre for Contextual Hermeneutics, 1987). Since Lategan

was the only Biblical scholar among the coauthors, it can be presumed that he wrote the passages challenging the Biblical authority for apartheid.

33. Bernard C. Lategan, "Intertextuality and Social Transformation: Some Implications of the Family Concept in New Testament Tests," in S. Draisma, *Intertextuality in Biblical Writings: Essays in Honour of Bas van Iersel* (Kampen: Kok, 1989), 115. The difference between *Church and Society* and the Kairos Document, according to one scholar, was that the latter, along with "The Road to Damascus," was more direct and far-reaching in its attack on apartheid in that it did not merely question the flawed application of apartheid but characterized apartheid as an inherently unjust and violent system. See Johann Kinghorn, "On the Theology of Church and Society in the DRC," *Journal of Theology for Southern Africa* 70 (March 1990): 21–36.

34. On this experience, see Bernard C. Lategan, "Some Remarks on the Pragmatic Thrust of Galatians 3:28," in Smit, *Hermeneutics and Social Transformation*, 79–89.

35. Bernard C. Lategan "Scholar and Ordinary Reader," in Smit, *Hermeneutics and Social Transformation*, 39–48, 44 (orig. pub. 1996). Lategan is drawing on M. Dube, "Readings of *Semoya*: Batswana Women's Interpretation of Matt. 15:21–28," *Semeia* 73 (1996): 111–29.

36. Lategan, "Scholar and Ordinary Reader," 44.

37. Lategan's ongoing account of Ricoeur's influence, already extensive, is still being elaborated. See Bernard C. Lategan, "Ricoeur in South Africa: Some Remarks on His Impact beyond Philosophy," *Stellenbosch Theological Journal* 4, no. 2 (2018): 113–34.

38. Lategan, "Mapping the Hermeneutical Process," in Smit, *Hermeneutics and Social Transformation,* 115–46, 126 (orig. pub. 2009); Paul Ricoeur, *Interpretation Theory: Discourse and the Surplus of Meaning* (Fort Worth: Texas Christian University Press, 1976), 75. Lategan also drew heavily on Paul Ricoeur, *Hermeneutics and the Social Sciences* (1981), and *Time and Narrative* (1984, 1985, 1988). The phrase "unintended readers" is from L. Hartman, "On Reading Others' Letters," *Harvard Theological Review* 79 (1986): 137–46. On the newly empowered role of the reader, see also Lategan, "Coming to Grips with the Reader" in Smit, *Hermeneutics and Social Transformation* (29–38), and "Current Issues in the Hermeneutical Debate."

39. This point is the conclusion of Lategan, "Current Issues in the Hermeneutical Debate," 27.

40. Lategan, "Mapping the Hermeneutical Process," 140. Interestingly, Greenblatt ran an ongoing seminar at the Wissenschaftskolleg zu Berlin on "cultural mobility" that describes the circulation of the text in society in just these terms. See Stephen Greenblatt, Ines Županov, Reinhard Meyer-Kalkus, Heike Paul, Pál Nyírí, and Friederike Pannewick, *Cultural Mobility: A Manifesto* (New York: Cambridge University Press, 2009). On "other readers," see Lategan, "Taking the Third Public Seriously," 149–58, and "Scholar and Ordinary Reader," 39–48, both in Smit, *Hermeneutics and Social Transformation.*

41. Dirk J. Smit, "Interpreter Interpreted: A Reader's Reception of Lategan's Legacy," in Breytenbach Thom, and Punt, *The New Testament Interpreted,* 3–25, 11. Smit tends to treat Lategan's oeuvre as exceptionally various but essen-

tially consistent with itself from the beginning, somewhat understating the turn in Lategan's thinking emphasized here.

42. Bernard C. Lategan, "Is Paul Defending His Apostleship in Galatians?," *New Testament Studies* 34 (1988): 411–30, 425. For a more detailed discussion of Lategan's thinking on this subject, see Breytenbach, "'Not according to Human Criteria,'" 57–58.

43. Lategan, "Reading the Letter to the Galatians," 139.

44. From http://stias.ac.za/news/2018/10/stias-appoints-edward-kirumira-as-new-director/.

3. VIRGIN VISION

1. See note 8.

2. Although Wallace manages the impressive feat of footnotes within footnotes, his contributions to the genre, while massive in scale (see no. 110, which occupies a full fifteen pages), ultimately disappoint because they lack the gladiatorial spirit: as endnotes, they abandon the field of the "main text" and set up camp safely behind the lines in the final pages.

3. Anthony Grafton, *The Footnote: A Curious History* (Cambridge, MA: Harvard University Press, 1997). According to Grafton, the footnote as a genre "flourished most brightly in the eighteenth century," when a spirit of irony and artistry produced, among others, Gibbon. In the melancholy nineteenth century, he continues, footnotes, "like so many Carmens . . . found themselves reduced to laborers and confined to a vast, dirty factory" (229).

4. The footnote explains that the Catholic Church envisioned the possibility that one might be christened before he is born: "*The Romish Rituals direct the baptizing of the child, in cases of danger, before it is born;—but upon this proviso, That some part or other of the child's body be seen by the baptizer:—But the Doctors of the Sorbonne, by a deliberation held amongst them, April 10, 1733,—have enlarged the powers of the midwives, by determining, That though no part of the child's body should appear,— that baptism shall, nevertheless, be administered to it by injection,—par le moyen d'une petite canulle,—Anglicè *a squirt.*" Laurence Sterne, *The Life and Opinions of Tristram Shandy Gentleman* (Hertfordshire: Wordsworth Editions, 1996), 41.

5. David Hume, *The History of England from the Invasion of Julius Caesar to the Rebellion of 1688,* vol. 2 (London: A. Millar, 1762), 251.

6. G. H. Martin, introduction to *Knighton's Chronicle, 1337–1396,* ed. and trans. G. H. Martin (Oxford: Clarendon Press, 1995), xxii–xl.

7. Grafton, *The Footnote,* 234. The publication Grafton refers to is given as "E. W[ind], 'Introduction,' *A Bibliography on the Survival of the Classics,* I (London, 1934), v–xii." It appears to be case, then, that this four-decker citational apparatus occupies just eight pages of text.

8. In fact, the semi-fictionalized account in the first pages of this chapter drew heavily on two texts by the same Linda Nochlin: "Not Too Far from Brooklyn: Growing Up, Growing Old with Art," ACLS Occasional Paper No. 64 (2008); and *Mathis at Colmar* (New York: Red Dust, 1963).

9. Maura Reilly, "A Dialogue with Linda Nochlin, the Maverick She," in *Women Artists: The Linda Nochlin Reader,* ed. Maura Reilly (New York: Thames and Hudson, 2015), 8–41, 8. This volume contains a comprehensive bibliography of Nochlin's writings; hereafter *WA.*

10. Among the scholars influenced by Nochlin are many of the contributors to *Self and History: A Tribute to Linda Nochlin,* ed. Aruna d'Souza (London: Thames and Hudson, 2001).

11. Linda Nochlin, *Gustave Courbet: A Study of Style and Society* (New York: Garland, 1976), 2, 3. This is the title given the dissertation when it was published in 1976 as part of a Garland series, Outstanding Dissertations in the Fine Arts. Nochlin's title was *The Development and Nature of Realism in the Work of Gustave Courbet: A Study of the Style and Its Social and Artistic Background.*

12. Ernst Gombrich describes the Isenheim Altar as an orthodox product of the medieval guild, saying that Grünewald "does not seem to have felt any doubts. Art for him . . . could have only one aim, the aim of all religious art in the Middle Ages—that of providing a sermon in pictures, of proclaiming the sacred truths as taught by the Church." Gombrich, *The Story of Art* (New York: Phaidon, 1951), 257. H. W. Janson (one of Nochlin's supervisors at NYU) comes to the opposite conclusion: "In a word, Grünewald seems to have shared the free, individualistic spirit of Italian Renaissance artists; the daring of his pictorial vision likewise suggests a reliance on his own resources." Janson, *History of Art: A Survey of the Major Visual Arts from the Dawn of History to the Present Day* (Englewood Cliffs, NJ: Prentice-Hall, 1964), 390.

13. Roger Fry, *Flemish Art: A Critical Survey* (London: Chatto and Windus, 1927); Clive Bell, *Flemish Art* (quoted in *WA*, 418); Clive Bell, *Art* (London: Chatto and Windus, 1914). Both quoted in *WA*, 418. Not all critics shared this view. Meyer Schapiro, who was teaching at Columbia when Nochlin was attending the Institute of Fine Arts in New York, would have been an inspiring model of fine-grained responsiveness, as well as a model for a sociohistorical understanding of art.

14. Linda Nochlin, "Women, Art, and Power," in Nochlin, *Women, Art, and Power* (New York: Harper and Row, 1988), 1–36, 33. This is the final form of a lecture Nochlin gave on many occasions.

15. Linda Nochlin, *Realism: Style and Civilization* (New York: Penguin Books, 1971), 43.

16. This dialogic relation, fundamental to what I have been describing as scholarship's generation of the new, became an articulate conviction later in Nochlin's career. In a 1999 essay, Nochlin says, "Original work (and thought) is invariably attained in dialogue with already existing work." Linda Nochlin, "Memoirs of an Ad Hoc Art Historian," in *Representing Women* (New York: Thames and Hudson, 1999), 6–33, 11.

17. In a 2014 essay on Ellen Altfest, Nochlin notes that "realism seems almost to have been invented as a way of indicating class difference. In the Middle Ages, irregularities, sordid details and lack of decorum were reserved for the representation of peasants, contrasting their low status with the elegantly idealized or decorative styles favored for aristos of heavenly figures." Nochlin, "Ellen Altfest: A New, New Realism," in *WA*, 417–25, 421.

18. See Linda Nochlin, "In Detail: Courbet's *Burial at Ornans*," in *Courbet* (New York: Thames and Hudson, 2007), 109–15. In a 2000 interview, Nochlin said that her dissertation on Courbet "unleashed a flow" of subsequent work on the political character of realism, naming in particular the work of T. J. Clark, which she described as "more complex, and more dialectical and more Marxist," without, however, being "any righter" than she had been. Linda Nochlin, "The Feminist Turn in the Social History of Art," interview with Richard Candida Smith, Art History Oral Documentation Project, J. Paul Getty Trust (2000), https://archive.org/stream /feministturninsooonoch/feministturninsooonoch_djvu.txt, p. 56. See T. J. Clark, *Image of the People: Gustave Courbet and the 1848 Revolution* (Princeton, NJ: Princeton University Press, 1984; orig. pub. 1973). Clark might not have been flattered to hear that he was part of the flow Nochlin considered herself to have unleashed. His 1973 book does not mention her, but explicitly takes issue with the thesis she advanced about Courbet's "compositional *égalitarisme*" in *A Burial at Ornans*. "Structure is what counts," he said there, "not detail; and looked at whole, the *Burial* is anything but hybrid" (*Image of the People*, 81). For another approach that discerns structure in Courbet's apparently haphazard composition, see Michael Fried, "The Structure of Beholding in *A Burial at Ornans*," in Fried, *Courbet's Realism* (Chicago: University of Chicago Press, 1990), 111–47.

19. See Nochlin's 1974 essay "Some Women Realists," in *WA*, 76–92; and "Ellen Altfest," in *WA*, 417–25 (2014).

20. Linda Nochlin, "Courbet, the Real Allegory," in *Courbet*, 6–18, 7.

21. She was far from alone in seeing a political dimension to Courbet's work. Her dissertation begins by listing several critics in the nineteenth century and scholars in the twentieth century who felt that Courbet's social and political outlook was central to his art, including Klaus Berger, Benedict Nicolson, and Meyer Schapiro. But none of these had been nearly as definite as she in identifying the Revolution of 1848 as the context, or in linking Courbet's style systematically to that context.

22. It should be noted that by focusing on the connection between art and politics in a dissertation submitted in 1963, Nochlin was taking her own professional risks in a professional milieu dominated by formalist analysis and an artistic milieu dominated by abstract expressionism. In fact, some may have discerned a rebellious intent even in her choice of realism as a subject. See Linda Nochlin, "The Realist Criminal and the Abstract Law," *Art in America* 61, no. 5 (1973): 54–61.

23. Nochlin, "Starting from Scratch: The Beginnings of Feminist Art History," *Women and Art,* 188–99, 188; reprinted in *WA,* 188–99.

24. See Linda Nochlin, "Courbet's *L'Origine du monde:* The Origin without an Original," in *Courbet,* 145–52; orig. pub. in *October* 37 (1986): 76–86. On occasion, Nochlin indicts not just art criticism but art itself as corrupted by the driving force of male desire, a force so powerfully entrenched that it has defined desire on its own terms: "What *men* want," she says, "is what want *is*; men's want defines desire itself." Linda Nochlin, "Courbet's Real Allegory: Rereading *The Painter's Studio,*" in Nochlin, *Courbet,* 153–85, 181.

25. Nochlin, "Why Have There Been No Great Women Artists?," in *WA*, 42–68. When it was published in *ARTnews* in January 1971, the essay served as the focal point for a special issue on feminism that included statements from Elaine de Kooning and Rosalyn Drexler (a dialogue), Marjorie Strider, Louise Nevelson, Lynda Benglis, Suzi Gablik, Eleanor Antin, and Rosemarie Castoro. Nochlin's field-founding intervention can be compared to that of Anne Firor Scott, whose *The Southern Lady: From Pedestal to Politics, 1830–1930* (Charlottesville: University of Virginia Press, 1970) came at the same moment and had an impact on Southern women's history comparable Nochlin's on feminist art history and criticism.

26. Linda Nochlin, "How Feminism in the Arts Can Implement Cultural Change," *Arts in Society* 2, no. 1–2 (Spring-Summer 1974): 80–89, 89.

27. Interview quoted by David Levering Lewis, *W. E. B. Du Bois: Biography of a Race, 1868–1919*, vol. 1 of 2 (New York: Henry Holt, 1993), 226.

28. E. H. Carr, *What Is History?* (New York: Vintage Books, 1961), 112.

29. Linda Nochlin, introduction to *Women, Art, and Power* (New York: Harper and Row, 1988), xi–xvi, xii–xiii. According to Nochlin, "A feminist art history is a transgressive and anti-establishment practice meant to call many of the major precepts of the discipline into question." See also Linda Nochlin, "'Why Have There Been No Great Women Artists?' Thirty Years After," in *WA*, 311–21, 320.

30. Linda Nochlin, "Courbet's Real Allegory," in Nochlin, *Courbet*, 153–85; first published in Sarah Faunce and Linda

Nochlin, *Courbet Reconsidered,* exhibition catalogue (New York: Brooklyn Museum, 1988). The painting was also the subject of pp. 210–25 in Nochlin, *Gustave Courbet: A Study of Style and Society.*

31. The identification of the figures on the left-hand side was the work of Hélène Toussaint, "A propos d'une critique," Les Amis de Gustave Courbet, *Bulletin* 61 (1979): 10–13; quoted in Nochlin, "Courbet's Real Allegory," 156–57. Figures include a supporter of Napoleon III, a Catholic journalist, an editor, an Italian associated with Garibaldi, a Hungarian insurgent; also Tadeusz Kościuszko, standing for the Polish freedom movement; and Bakunin, representing Russian socialism.

32. Klaus Herding, "Das *Atelier des Malers,*" in *Realismus als Widerspruch: Die Wirklichkeit in Courbets Malerei,* ed. K. Herding (Frankfurt am Main, 1978), 223–47.

33. Angus Fletcher, *Allegory: The Theory of a Symbolic Mode,* 2nd ed. (Princeton, NJ: Princeton University Press, 2012), 306; quoted in Nochlin, "Courbet's Real Allegory," 159. Fletcher actually goes much farther, describing the personality of the allegorical hero as rigid, anxious, and fatalistic, and even, in his monomania, suggesting "magical influence, psychic possession, taboo restrictions" (303).

34. As Nochlin notes, some theorists of allegory have identified this resistance to determinate meaning even within allegory, which, by overinterpreting details, liberates all signifiers "into polyvalence," as Terry Eagleton puts it in his discussion of Walter Benjamin. Terry Eagleton, *Walter Benjamin, or Towards a Revolutionary Criticism* (London: Verso, 1981), 20; quoted in Nochlin, "Courbet's Real Allegory," 166.

35. Hannah Arendt, *The Origins of Totalitarianism* (Orlando, FL: Harcourt, 1976).

36. Hannah Arendt, *The Human Condition* (Chicago: University of Chicago Press, 1958). "What Is Freedom?" was published in Arendt, *Between Past and Future: Eight Exercises in Political Thought* (New York: Penguin, 1977; orig. pub. 1961), 142–69.

37. On the miraculous character of action, see *The Human Condition:* "The miracle that saves the world . . . is ultimately the fact of natality, in which the faculty of action is ontologically rooted" (247); also "What Is Freedom?": "Every act, seen from the perspective not of the agent but of the process in whose framework it occurs and whose automatism it interrupts is a 'miracle'—that is, something which could not be expected" (168).

CONCLUSION

1. Anthony Grafton, *The Footnote: A Curious History* (Cambridge, MA: Harvard University Press, 1997), 233.

ACKNOWLEDGMENTS

Scholarship is not an easy subject to study, but it is a subject one can learn by doing. I have been instructed not only by personal experience but also by the many people I have known over the course of a long career in the profession, as I have never been comfortable calling it. This book is my thanks and tribute to all. I would, however, like to single out for special gratitude just a few whose contributions were unusual. I would owe a great debt to Joel Conarroe if all he had done was give me my first break, over forty years ago. But that was, as it turns out, the least of his gifts, and I dedicate the book to him. John Harpham—always my first, often my best, and sometimes my most expensive reader—keeps alive my faith in the future. I began thinking some of the thoughts presented here when I was asked to give a lecture at the Swedish Collegium for Advanced Study in Uppsala. I thank my friend Björn Wittrock, the Principal, for the invitation, and the various members of the audience who, with great politeness, pointed out the lecture's inadequacies and set me on the path whose end, for the moment, this book is. Also? Marie Lorena Moore, for the ongoing inspiration of her friendship. Finally, the book was completed at the Institut für die Wissenschaften vom Menschen in Vienna, and I wish to thank Shalini Randeria, Rector, for her kindness and hospitality during my time there.

INDEX

Academy. *See* Faculty; Higher
    education; Scholar; Universities
Action, 136–138, 179n37
Acts, Book of. *See* Bible.
African Americans: as Americans,
    15–16; Black Codes, 43; double
    consciousness of, 15, 16; education
    as good for, 20; emancipatory
    instrument of scholarship and,
    18–19; identity of, 15–16; lynching
    of, 42, 126; during Reconstruction,
    42–45; spending habits of, 149–150n1.
    See also Du Bois, W. E. B.
African National Congress, 88
Afrikaans language, 69
Afrikaners, 69–71, 163–164n18. *See*
    also Apartheid; Lategan,
    Bernard C.; South Africa
Albert, Hans, 160n6
Allegory, 130–131, 178nn31,33,34
Americans, African Americans as,
    15–16
Antony, Saint, 154n24
Apartheid: Belhar Confession, 78,
    168n29; Bible and, 166n24 (*see also*
    Lategan, Bernard C.; Paul's Letter
    to the Galatians); Broederbond
    (Brotherhood) and, 70; DRC and,

75–76, 77–78, 80, 167n26, 168n29;
end of, 88; Kairos Document, 78,
79, 169n33; Lategan's disaffection
with, 77; Lategan's suspicions
about moral character of, 80–82;
religion and, 72–74 (*see also*
Lategan, Bernard C.; Paul's Letter
to the Galatians); role of academia
in sustaining, 71; Verwoerd's definition of, 71. *See also* Lategan,
Bernard C.; South Africa
Appiah, Kwame Anthony, 40, 153n21
Arendt, Hannah, 134–137
Argumentation, footnotes and, 106
Art: depiction of women in, 119;
effects of, 96–97; ekphrasis, 111,
112–115; male desire and, 176n24;
Nochlin's definition of, 123–124;
Nochlin's exposure to, 93;
Romantic conception of, 123;
talent vs. situation, 124–125;
viewing with virgin vision, 115;
"Why Have There Been No Great
Women Artists?," 123–125
Art criticism / art history, 94, 128;
critique, 128–129; male desire
and, 176n24; social history and,
125. *See also* Feminist art

183